The
ULTIMATE
Kids' Club
Book

How to organize, find members, run meetings, raise money, handle problems, and much more!

Melissa Maupin

Edited by Rosemary Wallner

Library of Congress Cataloging-in-Publication Data

Maupin, Melissa, 1958–
The ultimate kids' club book: how to organize, find members, run meetings, raise money, handle problems, and much more! / by Melissa Maupin.
       p.   cm.
    Includes bibliographical references and index.
    Summary: Provides information on starting a club, with tips on organizing, finding members, electing officers, running meetings, raising money, and handling problems.
    ISBN: 1-57542-007-4
    1. Children — Societies and clubs — Handbooks, manuals, etc. — Juvenile literature. 2. Clubs — Handbooks, manuals, etc. — Juvenile literature. [1. Clubs — Handbooks, manuals, etc.] I. Title.
HS3258.M38   1996
367'. 068—dc20   96–13095
                                                      CIP
                                                      AC

Cover and book design by MacLean & Tuminelly
Index prepared by Eileen Quam and Theresa Wolner

10 9 8 7 6 5 4 3 2 1
Printed in the United States of America

Free Spirit Publishing Inc.
400 First Avenue North, Suite 616
Minneapolis, MN 55401-1730
(612) 338-2068
help4kids freespirit.com

Dedication

To my children, Mark and John Michael, who asked me to write this book. And to my husband, John, who always believed in me.

Acknowledgments

Thanks to all the kids who contributed their wonderful ideas to this book. A special thanks to Mrs. Dunk's class from Montclair Elementary School for their input and interesting club stories.

Contents

List of Reproducible Pages

Introduction

Have you ever spent an afternoon in front of the TV, bored out of your mind?

Is there a hobby or sport you'd like to try?

Do you come home from school wishing you had something to do?

Is there a problem in your neighborhood, town, or city you'd like to help solve?

Is Saturday "just another day" to you?

Is there a cause you'd like to support?

Is there something about yourself that you'd like to improve, but you're not sure how to start?

Would you like to learn a new skill?

Would you like to make new friends or have more fun with the friends you have?

If you answered "yes" to even one of these questions, then maybe you should start a club. If you're looking for ideas, suggestions, and tips, you've come to the right place.

This book tells you how to start and run a successful club in your neighborhood, apartment building, community center, place of worship, school, or anywhere else you choose. You'll learn:

- what to do first
- if and when to get a sponsor
- how to structure your club
- how to attract new members

- how to keep the members you have
- how to design a clubhouse without much money
- ways to make meetings more interesting
- how to raise money when you need it
- how to handle problems that sometimes arise
- and much, much more.

Many ideas in this book come from real kids who started real clubs. (Some of their clubs were successful, and others were total flops.) Throughout this book, they share stories and offer advice — from serious to silly.

Each chapter focuses on a particular part of club life — getting started, making plans, organizing, and so on. You'll find activities to try (with step-by-step instructions) and forms to copy and use. Special "Club Flub!" sections explore mistakes to avoid and explain how you can make a better decision or choice. "Trivia Tidbits" tell about different kinds of clubs and projects, from weird to hilarious.

If you already belong to a club, this book is for you, too. Flip through it for ideas on solving problems, making meetings more lively, jump-starting a tired club, and more.

You should know from the beginning that starting a club takes work. You're going to spend a lot of time and effort on getting it going and getting it right. Sometimes you might feel tired or frustrated. You might even ask yourself, "Why am I doing this?" At moments like these, it will help to remind yourself of the positive things a club can do for you. Here's just a sampling of the benefits you can expect from being part of a club:

- *Personal power.* When people join together, they can do things that individuals couldn't do on their own. That's because club members support and encourage each other. They combine ideas and resources as they reach for common goals.
- *A sense of belonging.* A club is a great way to hook up with others who share your interests and concerns. As a club member, you'll

be able to talk and play with old and new friends at every meeting. You'll share good times — and you'll help each other through tough times, too.

- ☉ *Places to go and things to do.* Forget about boredom! You'll be too busy.
- ☉ *Skills you need to succeed in life.* Governments and many businesses are run very much like clubs. Your club experiences will help you with whatever you do in your future. You'll gain leadership experience and learn a lot about cooperation, negotiation, organization, and money management.

"Clubs can really help you. If you have a problem, you can talk about your problem with friends in the club and find a solution." —Kimberly

Maybe you're wondering, "Why should I start a club? There are already plenty of clubs around that I could join." That's true, and maybe you should join one. It might be perfect for you. On the other hand, existing clubs might not offer what you need. Perhaps they focus on activities that don't interest you, or they meet at inconvenient times or places. Maybe you don't feel comfortable around the club members, or perhaps the club is run by adults with little chance for kids to lead. When you start your own club, you and your friends get to make the decisions. And your club can be just what you want it to be. Good luck and have fun!

Melissa Maupin
Corpus Christi, Texas

1

The Basics

What is a club? A club is a group of people linked together by a common purpose. Without people who are interested and willing to participate, a club is just an idea.

A club may be very small (three or four members who meet every week at someone's house). Or it may be very large (thousands of members from all over the world who meet once a year or belong to a smaller branch of the club in their city or town). A club can have another name: association, group, organization, circle, fellowship, society, or council.

Club members communicate with each other. Usually this happens at meetings, but some clubs share news and information in other ways. They produce newsletters, write letters, send E-mail, or talk on the phone.

Every club must have a purpose — a reason for being. This can be simple and broad ("to share fun adventures with other kids"), challenging and specific ("to learn French"), or anywhere in between.

What do you need to start a club?

1. An idea for a club.
2. Friends who might be interested in joining.
3. Enough free time to meet.

"My friend has a cabin playhouse in her backyard. I'd like to start a club there with about six other girls. We could call it 'The Kind Club.' The purpose of our club would be to try to find ways to help other people. We could help people in the neighborhood by doing chores and going to the store for them."
—Stephanie

On the next page, you'll find a "Club Plans" form you can copy and use to write down your plans for your club. Start by writing down your idea for your club. List the names of some friends you think might want to join. Then get together with them and read the rest of this chapter. Along the way, you can fill out the rest of the form — and you'll be on your way to starting your club.

Should your club be formal or informal?

A *formal* club has a regular meeting time and place. The meetings are run in an orderly way. Members of formal clubs usually join at the beginning of the club period and stay members for a certain length of time — for example, the school year. Formal clubs hold elections and choose officers.

An *informal* club might have a regular meeting time and place, or it might meet whenever and wherever possible. The meetings are looser and more casual. Members may meet just to talk, play, or work on a project. Informal clubs often allow new members to join at any time. They may or may not have officers or group leaders.

Decide what kind of club you'll have. Check either "Formal" or "Informal" on the "Club Plans" form.

 CLUB PLANS

Idea for club: _____

_____

_____

Friends who might want to join:

_____

_____

_____

We think our club should be ❏ Formal ❏ Informal

Where we think we want to meet: _____

_____

The supplies and equipment we think we will need:

_____

_____

The type of club we want to start is a: ❏ Home club
❏ Backyard club ❏ School club ❏ A club at our place of worship
❏ A club at our community center ❏ Other: _____

Do we need a sponsor? ❏ Yes ❏ No

Names of some possible sponsors:

_____

_____

Any other thoughts about our club: _____

_____

_____

_____

_____

TRIVIA TIDBITS
Strange-But-True Clubs!

Bald-Headed Men of America: Members believe that "bald is beautiful." They promote a National Rub-a-Bald-Head-Week and publish a newsletter called *Chrome Dome.*

Procrastinators' Club: Members believe in putting things off until later. They hold a Christmas party in June and a Fourth of July picnic in January.

Count Dracula Society: Teachers, writers, librarians, movie producers, and others join this club to study horror films and stories. The club maintains a Horror Hall of Fame and publishes *The Count Dracula Quarterly* newsletter.

Redheads International: Redheads in 30 countries belong to this group. They hold a Miss Redhead International Beauty Contest and publish the *Red Alert* newsletter.

What type of club should you start?

That depends on how you and your friends answer these questions:

- ❂ What will your club's purpose be?
- ❂ Will your club be formal or informal?
- ❂ What types of people do you hope will join?
- ❂ How much help and advice will you want?
- ❂ What kinds of facilities will you need? (A large meeting room? A gym? An outdoor area? A stage? Or just a corner in your home?)
- ❂ What supplies will you need? (Simple supplies like paper and pencils? Or more costly supplies like sports equipment, science equipment, a computer, art supplies, or special books?)

As you read the following descriptions, keep the "Club Plans" form on hand. You'll be writing down possible meeting places and times, listing supplies and equipment you'll need, and checking the type of club you want to start.

Home and backyard clubs

A club in your home or backyard is usually an informal organization of neighborhood kids. Members are friends, neighbors, and kids from school or your place of worship. When you start this type of club, think about where you'll meet. In the kitchen or basement? At a picnic table or backyard tree? Often you can get supplies for your club from things you already have (such as paper, pens, and stamps for a letter-writing club) and can share these supplies with other members. You can run this type of club without much adult help.

"My friend Amanda and I have a little garden club. We go out and find seeds and plant them in the backyard. Sometimes our other friends help us out." —Jordan

School clubs

A school club is usually more formal than a home or backyard club because members will need to know ahead of time when and where to meet. Members are from your class, grade, or different grade levels at your school. School clubs meet at a room in your school and usually have supplies on hand (such as computers for a computer club or books for a library club). Most school clubs have a sponsor or advisor (a teacher, coach, counselor, or parent). There may be rules about the kind of club you can start at your school. Ask a teacher if your club idea sounds like a good one and how you can get started.

CLUB FLUB!

You need to ask your principal's permission to start a club at your school. So you barge into her office one day with a vague sort of idea about your club and future plans.

Principals are busy people with many decisions to make each day and not much time to waste. Before you go into the office, talk to a teacher. Prepare an information sheet for your principal. Write your name at the top, then answer these questions:

1. What type of club are you planning?
2. Why is this a good club for your school?
3. What is the purpose of your club?
4. Do you have a sponsor or advisor?

If the principal is busy, you can leave the information sheet in the office, and the principal can look over your idea and get back to you later. If the principal isn't busy (TIP: make an appointment!), you can refer to the information sheet as you talk about your club. That way you'll keep your ideas straight, and you won't leave out anything important.

Place of worship and community center clubs

Clubs in a place of worship or community center can be either informal social groups or formal clubs. Many places of worship have organized youth programs. Ask the youth director if you can add your club to the program. Some places of worship have meeting rooms or other quiet areas where you can meet. Depending on your planned activities, you may have to bring supplies from home for your club. To get started, talk to the youth director or a clergy member about your club.

Often in a community center or recreation program, many children are involved in different activities at the same time. It may be difficult to get an adult to help you run your club, so you might want to think of a club you can run on your own. Once you've thought of a club, ask the center's director or youth leader for permission and guidance. In a community center or recreation program, space is sometimes limited — your club may have to meet at a table or in the corner of a room. You'll also have to bring your own supplies unless they're part of activities already available (such as board games or sports).

If you and your club members are in a supervised recreation program, try a club that focuses on an activity you normally do there like arts and crafts or board games. You'll already have the space and the supplies. Free play time or lunchtime may be a good opportunity for your club to meet.

"We had a club last summer at our recreation program. The recreation program was at our school in the cafeteria. On the last day, we put on a talent show. I danced in the show. The coaches picked a queen and king and crowned them." —Hope

Do you need a sponsor for your club?

A sponsor — also known as an advisor or director — is an adult who offers guidance, advice, and support to your club. A sponsor can order materials, store money and supplies, and help with problems you might not be able to solve on your own. You'll need a sponsor if you form a school club or other formal club. You usually don't need one for a home, backyard, or community center club.

A sponsor can be a teacher, parent, neighbor, or other responsible adult. When choosing a sponsor, look for someone who believes in the idea of your club, is interested in your club, and has the time to help. List possible sponsors for your club on the "Club Plans" form.

Pick one person from your list and invite him or her to be your sponsor. Describe your club's type and purpose. Explain when and where you'll be meeting. If that person is not able to sponsor your club, ask someone else from your list. Or see if that person can recommend another possible sponsor for your club.

If you choose not to have a sponsor, it's still a good idea to think of adults who can help you if you need it.

How to write your club charter

A charter makes your club official. It's a fun and easy way to organize and record important information about your club. On the next page, you'll find a "Club Charter" form you can copy and use. Read on to find out about club names, mottoes, pledges, and laws.

Picking a name

Most clubs pick a name that tells something about them. A cooking club might call themselves "The Junior Chefs" or "Let's Cook Club." You might choose to use a silly or nonsense name. For example, a neighborhood sports club might decide to call themselves the "Maple Street Maniacs."

Or you can use an acronym for your club name. An acronym is a set of initials that spell a real or nonsense word. Many clubs use acronyms because their names are long or the acronyms are catchy and easy to remember.

To create an acronym, try this method: First, describe your club in a few words. Second, try different combinations until the first letters of the words spell something. If your club collects and trades comic books, take the *c*, *a*, and *t* from *collects and trades* to make the acronym C.A.T.

Once you've chosen a name, write it on your charter. Then enter the date so you'll always remember the day your club began. List the names of the founding club members.

⋆☆ CLUB CHARTER ☆⋆

This document certifies that the _____
                                            (NAME OF CLUB)

_____

was started on _____
                          (DATE)

Founding Members:

_____

_____

_____

_____

Our Motto: _____

_____

Our Pledge: _____

_____

_____

_____

Our Laws: _____

_____

_____

_____

_____

Paste your
emblem here.

TRIVIA TIDBITS

National Clubs with Acronyms for Names

CARE (Cooperative for American Relief Everywhere)

GASP (Group Against Smokers' Pollution)

NASCAR (National Association for Stock Car Auto Racing)

WHOA! (Wild Horse Organized Assistance)

Creating a motto

A motto is a short, catchy phrase that defines your club or its purpose. Like the Cub Scout motto "Do Your Best," yours should be brief and easy to remember. Mottoes are similar to slogans, which advertisers use to sell products and services. Pay attention to TV commercials and magazine ads and see if you can spot the slogans.

When you create your motto, think of your club as a product. What is it about your club that appeals to you and other members? Once you've created your motto, write it on your charter.

Writing a pledge

A pledge or promise expresses your loyalty to your club, its members, and its purpose. At each meeting, club members may stand and repeat the pledge, or you may just want new members to memorize it and repeat it when they join.

A pledge is usually longer than a motto. An example is the KSE Promise of the Kids for Saving Earth club. (To find out more about KSE, see page 30.)

The earth is my home.
I promise to keep it
healthy and beautiful.
I will love the land,
the air, the water,
and all living creatures.
I will be a defender
of my planet.
United with friends,
I will save the earth.

To create your pledge, think of answers to these questions:

◉ What is the main purpose of your club?

◉ What good things will your club do?

◉ What can each member do to help the club succeed?

Use the answers to write your pledge. To make your pledge easy to remember and fun to say, try making it rhyme. Ask each member to create a rhyming or non-rhyming pledge. When everyone is finished, vote on which pledge members like best and write it on your club charter.

Making club laws

Laws are designed to keep order in our communities and country. They exist to help and protect everyone. People who break laws generally have to pay the consequences.

Club laws are guidelines that keep your club running smoothly. Usually there are no consequences for breaking club laws. Members join or leave of their own free will.

Work together to decide on a few short, simple laws that everyone agrees to follow. For example:

1. Members will try to attend all meetings.
2. Members will be loyal to each other and work to get along.
3. Members will take care of and share club property.

Write your laws on your charter. Later you can add an emblem to make your charter even more official-looking. You'll find ideas for creating an emblem on page 82.

"Every summer we start this club with about four boys and sometimes one girl. We make up rules and rewards like the ones we have at school. Some of our rules are: no fighting, no tearing up the clubhouse, and no making fun of other people."
—John

Choosing the Purpose of Your Club

What will your club's main activity be? What is your focus? If you don't already know — or if you're searching for new activities or a different direction — look through these suggestions. Although the projects are listed under club types, many are flexible and may work for any type of club, so be sure to read the whole chapter for ideas.

Home and backyard clubs

In your home or backyard club, you may choose to work on hobbies, practice sports, strive for self-improvement, or help others. Following are ideas that don't require much money or other resources — just your own desire and energy.

Collectors' club

You may already be a collector, so share that passion with others. Join together and pool your special collection into one large set, or work together on your individual collections. Use meeting times to create display racks, cases, or booklets. Exchange items and information with club members and attend swap meets in your area.

What do collectors collect? Anything and everything! Some people collect aluminum foil and create giant foil balls. Others save comic books, marbles, or gumball machine prizes. You might collect stamps, thimbles, dolls, rocks, shells, autographs, or anything else that interests you and the other members of your club.

TRIVIA TIDBITS

What's in a Name?

Philately is the hobby of stamp collecting.

Conchologists collect shells.

Numismatics is the hobby of collecting and studying coins and money.

Lapidaries collect and study gemstones.

Coin collecting

Coin collecting is one of the oldest hobbies in the world. People began collecting coins sometime during the 17th century B.C., just after coins were invented. Search through your change, and maybe you'll stumble on a rare find. For help starting your collection, look through books on coin collecting or talk to other collectors.

Read more about it

Let's Collect Coins by Ken Bresset (Racine, WI: Western Publishing Company, 1991).

How to Make an Egg Carton Display Case

It's easy to make a display case out of an egg carton. You can use the case for small items like shells, rocks, or thimbles. You'll need an empty egg carton, construction paper, glue or tape, markers, old magazines, scissors, facial tissue or cotton balls, 1 1/2" squares of paper, and a pen or pencil.

1. Glue or tape a piece of construction paper over the egg carton's outside writing.

2. Open the carton. If the inside of the top has writing, tape or glue construction paper over it.

3. If you want, draw pictures on the outside and inside that go with your collection — like a beach scene for a shell collection — or cut out pictures from magazines to decorate your display case.

4. Line each of the egg holders with facial tissue or cotton balls.

5. Place your collected items in the egg holders.

6. Make identification labels by writing the name of each item on a small square of paper. Glue or tape your labels to the backs of the egg holders.

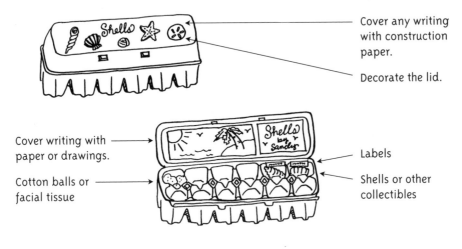

Cover any writing with construction paper.

Decorate the lid.

Cover writing with paper or drawings.

Cotton balls or facial tissue

Labels

Shells or other collectibles

Card collecting

Collecting sports cards, especially baseball cards, is one of the most popular hobbies today with over one million people participating. When you're collecting, try to find the card from a player's rookie year, since that card is more valuable than the player's star card. Instead of baseball cards, you may choose to collect other sports cards or cards of comic book superheroes, cartoon characters, television stars, or movie stars.

Read more about it

Baseball Cards, Questions, and Answers, edited by Mark K. Larson (Iola, WI: Krause Publications, 1992).

Arts and crafts club

You don't have to be a great artist to enjoy working with your hands and creating things. Anyone can learn a craft. If you walk through a craft or hobby store, you'll be amazed at the wide range of crafts available. You'll see kits and supplies for embroidery, wood painting, cloth painting, beadwork, stained glass, weaving, model making, and many others. You can also find books and magazines to guide you through projects.

Read more about it

The Kids Multicultural Art Book by Alexandra M. Terzian (Charlotte, VT: Williamson Publishing, 1993).

101 Things to Make by Juliet Bawden (New York: Sterling Publishing Company, 1994).

A Collage of Crafts by Charlie Guerrier (New York: Ticknor & Fields, 1994).

CLUB FLUB!

You want to start a greeting card club. You go to a nearby craft store, grab a cart, and load up on paper, paintbrushes and paint, markers, stamps and ink, glitter, and stickers. When you get to the check-out lane – uh oh! The total cost for everything in your cart is more money than you have.

It's easy to overspend on items you don't really need. Shop smart! Before you go to the store:

- Vote on what type of craft your club wants to try first.
- Check out supplies you already have at home; use club meetings to share supplies with other members.
- Decide how much money club members want to spend on supplies.
- Look in the newspaper for coupons and sales ads.

Found art

Found art is made from discarded items — free craft supplies! You can build sculptures with wire, bolts, nuts, and pieces of aluminum foil. Boxes, used wrapping paper, plastic bottles, aluminum cans, and pieces of string and ribbon can all be turned into interesting art pieces.

Ask your parents to give you interesting things they might otherwise throw away. See if your neighbors have other items you can use to create found art. IMPORTANT: Never go through anyone's trash or recycling bins without permission and adult supervision.

Art from the earth

Look outside and you'll find all kinds of free items that you can turn into beautiful crafts. Make sand paintings or pebble pictures. Weave yarn between sticks for a wall hanging. Search the beach or a forest for sticks, stones, rocks, and shells to make collages or to decorate boxes. Brush paint or ink on leaves, feathers, or shells and press them on paper to make nature prints.

Games club

Set up games — like horseshoes, badminton, and tetherball — in your backyard or a nearby park. Have club members play the games in a certain order or for a certain amount of time. Use garbage cans, lawn chairs, boxes, tires, and play equipment to create an obstacle course. Have club members run the course and keep time. Keep score as to who can complete the obstacle course in the shortest amount of time, or while hopping on one foot or using only one hand.

For an ongoing activity, design a crazy nine-hole miniature golf course using bricks and boards for ramps, plastic tubing for tunnels, and plastic cups for the holes. Trees, lawn chairs, and a garden hose make good obstacles. Play the course with a croquet set, toy golf set, or hockey sticks and tennis balls. Compete for the championship or charge a quarter to neighborhood kids to earn money for your club.

Read more about it

The World's Best Street & Yard Games by Glen Vecchione (New York: Sterling Publishing, 1989).

Hopscotch, Hangman, Hot Potato, & Ha Ha Ha: A Rulebook of Children's Games by Jack Maguire (New York: Prentice Hall, 1990).

New Rules for Classic Games by R. Wayne Schmittberger (New York: John Wiley & Sons, 1992).

Helping hands club

Put your bikes to a good use by starting a bicycle brigade. Ask to run errands or pick up items at a nearby store for neighbors who may need the extra help. Or brighten the day for someone who is alone or lonely by visiting once a week. Ask to help out around the house or just talk and play games.

Inventors' club

Put your heads together and invent a whatchamacallit or a super widget. Come up with a creative way to solve a common problem or make people's lives easier. Who knows? Your club could invent a better mousetrap and get rich! At your library, you'll find all kinds of books to inspire you to invent.

Read more about it

Experimenting with Inventions by Robert Gardner (New York: Franklin Watts, 1990).

Girls and Young Women Inventing by Frances A. Karnes and Suzanne M. Bean (Minneapolis, MN: Free Spirit Publishing, 1995).

Steven Caney's Invention Book by Steven Caney (New York: Workman Publishing, 1985).

The great exchange club

Exchange music, videos, or games. Make a countdown list of your club's favorite songs and perform them in lip-synching routines. Share movies or record and watch new TV shows together. Play a different board game at each meeting. Use an exchange system with check-out cards to keep track of borrowed items.

How to Start an Exchange System for Music, Books, Videos, or Games

Decide which items are "borrowable." Who wants to contribute cassettes, CDs, books, videos, or games to the exchange system? Will you keep the items in a central location (one member's house, a locker at school, a special box at your community center), or will members borrow items and return them to their owners? Once you have answered these questions, you're ready to start your exchange system. You'll need a set of 4" x 6" index cards and someone to take charge of them.

1. Create a check-out card for each item. Follow the example shown below or invent your own system.

2. Give club members a certain amount of time to borrow an item — two weeks is reasonable. They can renew their borrowing period for another two weeks if no one else is waiting for the item. This gives everyone the chance to borrow popular tapes, books, etc.

3. When a member borrows an item, he or she signs and dates the check-out card and leaves it with the member in charge of the cards.

4. When the borrower returns the item, the person in charge crosses out the borrower's name on the check-out card.

Item or Title: The Ultimate Kids' Club Book	
Member's Name	Date Checked Out (Must be returned in two weeks)
Bobby	March 12

CLUB FLUB!

You loaned your sister's favorite mystery book to a member of your mystery readers' club. The club member lost the book. Now your sister wants it back.

When you're looking for items to exchange in your club, use books, videos, magazines, or other things that members have brought to share or bought with club money. Ask parents, siblings, and others if they would like to donate items to your exchange club.

Before you start exchanging, have members write their names and phone numbers on all of their items in ink or permanent marker. At your meetings, look over the check-out cards and make sure items are returned on time. Track down anything that doesn't show up on the day it's due — and decide ahead of time what to do if someone loses or damages an item.

School clubs

School clubs are often related to subjects you are studying, but they're more fun than sitting in class. You get to choose the activities, and there aren't any tests or homework assignments. If you form a math club, for example, you could work on math puzzles and games or train for group math competitions. Many school clubs also focus on fitness and self-improvement, or sharpen skills such as acting or playing a musical instrument. Following are examples of clubs that work well in a school setting.

Welcome club

Moving to a new school can be scary. A "welcome" club can make new students feel more comfortable. Ask your principal to help you organize an information packet for new students. You could include a map of the school, a list of clubs to join, a school directory, and fun facts and trivia about your school. Club members could give new kids a tour of your school, introduce them to others, and stay with them during recess and lunchtime for the first few days or until they know their way around.

Second language club

There are many good reasons to learn a second language, and a school club is the perfect place to learn and practice new words and phrases.

Start by deciding which language your club wants to work on. Maybe one or more of the members knows a second language, or maybe you're already learning one at school. When you have made your choice, find a dictionary of that language at a library. (Your club might want to invest in a good paperback dictionary so you always have it available.) Start by learning basic phrases you use at every meeting — "hello," "goodbye," "please," "thank you," "let's get started," "any questions?" and so on — then challenge members to always say those phrases in the second language.

Decide how many new words or sentences you want to learn and practice at each meeting. Ask a teacher or sponsor for help in creating study sheets and audiocassettes. Find other kids at your school who know the language and invite them to give mini-lessons at your meetings. Find a local restaurant that serves food from the country whose language you're learning; plan to eat a meal there and order in your new language.

"We have a reading club that meets at the school library. Our teacher suggests a book, and then we all check it out or buy it. We have about fifteen kids in the club, and we all read the same book at the same time. It's exciting to talk about what's going on in the book. Our last book we read was A Day No Pigs Would Die, *which was good but gross.*

"We had a sleepover at our sponsor's house and took turns reading a book out loud. That was fun. And at the Christmas party, our sponsor gave us books. We had refreshments and made a huge mess with popcorn everywhere." —Tiffany

Etiquette club

The word *etiquette* is believed to come from 17th-century France. At that time, every member of the French court was given a long list or ticket (*etiquette,* in French) that told them how to behave on every social occasion.

Although our lives aren't as formal anymore, good manners and proper etiquette are still important. Find a book on manners and practice different situations during club meetings. Show off your new skills at a club dance or luncheon for your teachers or parents.

Read more about it

A Pocket Book of Manners for Young People by Elizabeth Hammond (Larkspur, CA: Trotwood Press, 1990).

Miss Best's Etiquette for Young People by Alyse Best (Portland, OR: Portland Entertainment Publishing, 1990).

Tutors and study buddies club

Create a tutoring club that meets after school once a week. Members could volunteer to help younger students with their schoolwork. You could also form a study buddy club and have members meet before or after school to study together and work on long-range assignments or school-wide projects.

Peaceful people club

Promote kind acts and do something nice for someone else at each meeting. Or ask your school to help you start a peer mediation program, in which club members help solve other kids' problems by listening to both sides and finding a fair solution.

Safety club

Start a club that lets others know about safety issues at home and school. Organize a bicycle obstacle course to teach bike safety in your school. Start a helmet promotional campaign for bicyclists and skaters by making posters and becoming good role models for others. Ask your local fire and emergency professionals for tips and information on fire prevention and water safety.

Don't smoke! club

Many kids get hooked on cigarettes as a result of peer pressure. Start an anti-smoking club and campaign for clean and healthy lungs. For information and help, write to:

American Lung Association
GPO #596-RB
New York, NY 10019

Ask about free and low-cost activity books for kids.

Place of worship and community center clubs

A club in your place of worship may focus on a variety of topics, including religious study, recreation, or helping others. A community center club can also focus on recreation or helping others in the community. Following are ideas to get you thinking about what type of club is right for you.

Clubs with a cause

You hear about the many problems in the world from TV programs, newspapers, and school classes. You might wonder what you can do to help. One of the best ways to begin solving a problem is to start in your neighborhood. Read the newspaper, watch the news, and talk to parents and teachers about local happenings. What local problems bother you the most? How could your club make a difference? Ask a sponsor or adult to help you research a topic, brainstorm ways to solve a problem, raise money, and carry out a solution.

Read more about it

The Kid's Guide to Service Projects: Over 500 Service Ideas for Young People Who Want to Make a Difference by Barbara A. Lewis (Minneapolis, MN: Free Spirit Publishing, 1995).

Start a drive

A drive is an organized effort to get people to donate items to others who need them. People often organize canned food drives or coat drives during the winter, but there is a need for drives throughout the year.

Perhaps your club could start a kids' clothing drive. Children grow out of clothes and shoes quickly, and often the items are still in good shape. Start by contacting a homeless shelter or your local

Goodwill store and ask if they need kids' clothes and shoes. If the answer is yes (and it probably will be), ask your parents to help you gather clothes that don't fit you anymore. Collect other clothes and shoes from neighbors. Decide on a place to bring all of the donated items. Sort them, make any needed repairs, clean them, and fold them. When you're ready, contact the shelter or Goodwill and arrange for the donated items to be picked up or delivered.

Your club could also start a toy and book drive for kids. Fix and clean up your old toys. With a parent, go through your books and sort out the ones you no longer want or need. Make posters advertising your toy and book drive and display them at your place of worship or community center. (Be sure to include information about where people can drop off their donated items.) Box the items and donate them to a local shelter.

Help the earth

If you're concerned with environmental issues, your club can help by finding ways to clean up your city or town. With help from a sponsor, use club meeting time to pick up trash on streets, along curbs, and in vacant lots. Volunteer your club to help clean up the water and shores of a local river, creek, or beach. Many communities have "adopt a street" programs, which means that your club would be responsible for cleaning that street on a regular basis. Graffiti is a problem in most cities, so ask business owners or the city to provide paint, and volunteer your artistic skills to design and paint murals over graffiti.

In 1990, a boy named Clinton Hill started Kids for Saving Earth, a club that helps clean up and protect the environment. Clinton died of cancer when he was just 11 years old, but his dream lives on through his club, which is now worldwide. To start a local branch club of Kids for Saving Earth, you'll need an adult advisor. For more information, write to:

Kids for Saving Earth Worldwide
P.O. Box 421118
Minneapolis, MN 55442

Nose for news club

Share good news and serious concerns by reporting them in a newsletter for your community center or place of worship. You'll probably need a sponsor or youth director to help you with this project. Ask your helper what type of equipment is available to you. A computer, for example, is great for writing and designing a newsletter. But you can also make one by hand or use a typewriter.

As reporters, you and the other club members could take notes at events and write stories. You might interview a member of the clergy, a community leader, or another interesting person in your neighborhood. Illustrate your stories with drawings or photographs. Ask your sponsor to make copies of your newsletter, then post them on bulletin boards at your community center or place of worship. Hand out copies to other kids.

Sports and games club

Almost any sport or game is a good reason for starting a club — softball, jump rope, in-line skating, croquet, Ping-Pong, twirling, checkers, dance, basketball, and just about anything else you can think of. Especially if you enjoy a sport or game that isn't usually offered at your school or community center, this is a great opportunity to have fun and share your interest with friends.

Community centers and places of worship often have recreation facilities and equipment that your club may be able to use. Check with the recreation director at your community center, or the youth director at your place of worship.

If your community doesn't have an organized sports program, you may want to set up friendly competitions within your club or with other clubs. On pages 32–34 are two ways to arrange competitions. (These tournaments will also work for board games, yard games, and card game challenges.)

Ladder tournament

You'll need a piece of lined paper, a pencil with an eraser, and as many slips of paper as you have players. If you have 10 players, number the lined paper from 1—10. Then number the slips of paper from 1—10, fold them, and put them in a box or a hat. Everyone draws a slip of paper.

On the numbered sheet of paper, fill in the players' names beside the numbers they drew. This is your "ladder." Don't worry if you end up on the bottom "rung." The names will shift as competition begins.

Anyone can challenge the person one or two "rungs" above him or her. If the challenger wins the competition, the names trade places on the "ladder." If the challenger loses, the names stay where they are.

The player on the top "rung" can challenge anyone else on the ladder. If he or she loses, the names trade places.

1. Hayley
2. Anna
3. Jackie
4. T.J.
5. Karen
6. Blair

In this example, T.J. can challenge either Jackie or Anna.

What happens if the competition continues for a while but the people on the top and bottom "rungs" aren't moving? To keep members interested, have the bottom and top players trade places. This gives everyone the chance to be a challenger.

Round robin tournament

In a round robin tournament, everyone plays everyone else once. The player or team with the most victories at the end is the champion.

You'll need a piece of paper and a pencil. If your club has 6 members, you'll each play 5 rounds of competition. On the paper, write "Round 1," "Round 2," "Round 3," "Round 4," and "Round 5," leaving room for names.

Under "Round 1," list three pairs of players. It doesn't matter who plays who first, since you'll all play every other member. Example:

ROUND 1

Kevin vs. Liz

Lynn vs. John

Kris vs. Sarah

After Round 1, rotate the names like this . . .

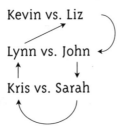

. . . so Round 2 looks like this:

ROUND 2

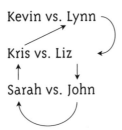

IMPORTANT: The first name in the left-hand column ALWAYS stays in the same place. All of the other names rotate in the way shown above.

Here's how the other rounds of this tournament would look:

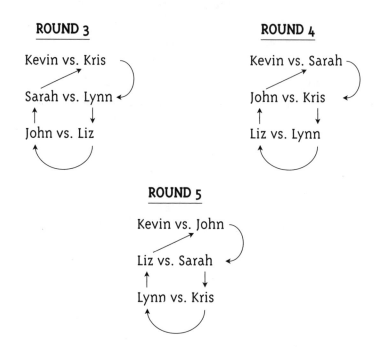

ROUND 3

Kevin vs. Kris

Sarah vs. Lynn

John vs. Liz

ROUND 4

Kevin vs. Sarah

John vs. Kris

Liz vs. Lynn

ROUND 5

Kevin vs. John

Liz vs. Sarah

Lynn vs. Kris

As you can see, a round robin tournament allows for a lot of play. But it might be too complicated and time-consuming if your club has many members.

3

The First Meeting

What's the key to a long-lasting, fun club? *Organization.* Use your first club meeting to welcome prospective members, organize yourselves, and decide the purpose of your club (get ideas from chapter 2). Set a place for people to meet (it doesn't have to be your permanent club headquarters, just somewhere convenient for most kids). Pick an exact meeting time and get the word out.

Four ways to announce your new club

1. *Word of mouth.* Simply telling everyone you know about your new club is an effective way to spread the news. For a home or backyard club, this may be all you need to do.

2. *Announcement.* For a school club, ask your principal if you can use the intercom to announce your meeting.

3. *Bulletin boards.* Many local stores, community centers, and places of worship have bulletin boards people use to post announcements. Ask the person in charge if you can post your club meeting notice.

4. *Flyers.* Hand out flyers door to door. Secure them to the doorknobs with rubber bands so they'll stay in place. (Ask your sponsor or another adult to go with you.)

Ben Franklin's Club

Benjamin Franklin was a great organizer. He started his career by organizing a club called the Junto, which met each week. The members set goals to own their own businesses, help their city (Philadelphia) grow, and make it a better place to live. Some of the Junto's accomplishments included starting a college, library, fire company, hospital, and insurance company. They also worked to pave, clean, and light the city streets, and formed a militia to protect the citizens.

Introducing your club

Once the prospective members have gathered, you'll need to tell them all about your club. Let them know its purpose and what the members will do together. Show them the club charter and explain the name, motto, and pledge. (You can all memorize and practice the pledge, if you like.) Show them the club laws and explain why they should follow them.

The membership roster

Bring a loose-leaf or spiral notebook to the first meeting. Write the club name on the front and keep it for the club notebook. The first page will be a list of members. To make this list, or roster, pass around the notebook or the sheet of paper and a pen or pencil. Have all the members print their names and telephone numbers on it. (Phone numbers are important so you can reach members to set special meetings or change plans.)

When and how to vote

Voting is so important to any club's success that it's a basic all members should know about right away. Voting is a tool for group decision making. You can vote on new club laws, different places to meet, or club projects. In order to get things done, you'll need to come to a general consensus, or agreement, about these and other issues.

There are two voting rules:

1. Everyone gets only one vote.
2. Everyone must accept the majority rule — the decision that most members want.

There are three ways to vote: the group voice vote, the show-of-hands vote, and the secret ballot.

"Sometimes it's hard for kids to get along and make decisions in a club. I've seen some get mad and quit because they didn't get their way." —Kerre

The group voice vote

A group voice vote is a quick and easy way to find out how everyone feels about an issue. Use this method when you're voting on only one issue. For example, one member may want to use the club money to buy sodas and chips for the next meeting. To find out if everyone agrees, call for a vote by asking, "Who's for spending our money on sodas and chips?" Those who like this idea say "Yes" or "Aye." (*Aye* is pronounced *eye*.)

Then ask, "Who's against spending our money on sodas and chips?" Those who don't like the idea say "No" or "Nay." (*Nay* is pronounced how it looks). Usually you can tell by the number of voices whether the idea is accepted or not. If it's too close to call, try voting with a show of hands.

The show-of-hands vote

A show-of-hands vote is another way to get a general group opinion, but it's more precise than the group voice vote. You've probably already used this method in your classroom or when playing with a group of your friends.

To use the show-of-hands vote, follow these steps:

1. Everyone offers ideas and the group talks about them.
2. When the group narrows down the ideas to two or three, you vote.
3. One person calls out the ideas one at a time.
4. Members raise their hand for the idea they want, and one person counts the hands. The idea that receives the most raised hands is the majority rule.

CLUB FLUB!

Your club is voting with a show of hands. You vote "yes" to having a club car wash to raise money ... but then you notice that your best friend is voting "no." So you change your vote.

The whole point of voting is to find out how everyone really feels about a question or issue. Stand by your beliefs when voting, even if you stand alone. Don't change your vote just because someone else's hand goes up or down.

The secret ballot

Use a secret ballot when club members want their decisions to be private. For example, you might use this method when there's a big disagreement about a decision, or when some members feel they have to side with a friend. Always use a secret ballot when voting for officers (see page 59 for making secret official ballots).

You'll need small slips of paper and a pen or pencil for each club member; a container to put the votes in, such as a bowl or hat; and a sheet of paper to tally the votes on. When it's time to vote, follow these steps:

1. Everyone writes his or her choice on a slip of paper, folds it, and places it in the container.

2. On the sheet of paper, one person writes down all the ideas that members are voting on. Another person reads each slip of paper and tallies the vote by writing a mark for every vote beside the idea. If you have a large group, write the votes in sets of five for easy counting. Here's an example:

Meet in Kimberly's basement ||

Meet in Jason's tree house ||

Meet in Mischa's living room ⊬⊬⊦

3. The two people add the marks and see which idea has the most votes — the majority rule. The counters should double-check the tally marks and totals to make sure the results are correct.

Setting your club goals

Now that your club is official and has members, it's time to think as a group and plan what you want to accomplish. Many people find it helpful to set goals for themselves. Writing goals down is important because it makes them real and easier to pursue. When you record your club's goals, you can check them from time to time to make sure they're still what your club wants. You can also make sure your club is on the right track.

Some members may not understand what you mean by goals. Start by explaining the difference between long-term and short-term goals and giving examples.

Long-term goals

Long-term goals are the ones your club wishes to achieve over three months, six months, a year, or just over the summer, depending on what type of club you have. Long-term goals can be simple, such as learning to play a different game every month, or they can be complicated, such as planning a drive to raise $1,000 for a charity.

Long-term goals should fit the purpose and structure of your club and should be realistic. At first you might not know if your goals are too difficult to achieve. If you think they are, ask your sponsor or another adult for advice on how to scale them down. But don't worry too much. Since you don't plan on reaching these goals right away, you can adjust them if necessary as you go along.

Short-term goals

Short-term goals are ones to work on during the next few meetings. Your short-term goals can be building blocks for your long-term goals, or they can be separate. For example, if your long-term goal is to build a clubhouse, a short-term goal might be to compare prices at local lumberyards or building-supply centers.

Pick an intriguing short-term goal that members can enjoy striving toward and achieve within the next few weeks. This will keep them interested in attending meetings.

TRIVIA TIDBITS
A Heavenly Goal

In 1887, astronomers from 18 observatories around the world met at the Paris Observatory. They left with a single goal: *Carte de ciel,* which meant *To map the heavens* (or record all the stars in the sky). Although their work ended in 1914, they managed to map over 2.5 million stars. The information they gathered is still used by astronomers today.

Brainstorming goals

Now that everyone knows about long-term and short-term goals, it's time to develop some goals for your club. Different members may have ideas about what they want to do in the future — and you probably have a few of your own, too. To find the best ideas, do a bit of brainstorming. You'll need a sheet of paper and a pen or pencil. Before you begin, review the four rules of brainstorming:

1. *Everyone who wants to contribute is welcome to contribute.* The more people thinking of ideas, the better.

2. *Write down every idea.* Ask everyone to come up with as many ideas as they can — from the silliest to the most serious.

3. *Accept every idea.* You can make your choices later.

4. *No criticizing.* Everyone is free to offer any idea that comes to mind.

Finalizing your goals

After your brainstorming session, read through all of the ideas. Talk about and vote on the ones members want to keep. Narrow the choices down to three or four for each category (short-term and long-term). Then record your goals. On page 42, you'll find a "Club Goals" form you can copy and use. Keep the filled-out form in the club notebook along with the club charter and membership roster.

"In my Odyssey of the Mind group, we brainstorm. It's weird. We will all be thinking silently. Everyone will be trying to come up with an idea. Then someone will say, 'I know!' That person will say something, and it gives you another idea. Then you say something and another person gets an idea and then another and another. Sometimes the things kids say are crazy. But that's okay. Crazy is creative." —J.M.

 # CLUB GOALS

Our Long-Term Goals (three to six months):

1. _____
   _____
   _____

2. _____
   _____
   _____

3. _____
   _____
   _____

4. _____
   _____
   _____

Our Short-Term Goals (the next two to three meetings):

1. _____
   _____
   _____

2. _____
   _____
   _____

3. _____
   _____
   _____

4. _____
   _____
   _____

Deciding on dues

Some clubs charge dues — money members pay to belong to the club. Members pay the dues when they first join the club, at every meeting, or once a year — whatever the club decides. The dues are collected and put in the treasury, and members vote on when and how to use the money. Some clubs publish a newsletter or pay for meeting space, and money from dues cover these expenses. Other clubs use dues to buy supplies or treats.

Should your club charge dues? That depends on the kind of club you have and what you need to pay for or purchase. For example, if your tie-dye club needs buckets, dyes, and rubber bands, you probably will want to charge dues. Propose an amount (keep it small!) and let the group vote.

CLUB FLUB!

Your club dues are 50 cents per meeting. At the first meeting, most people pay but some complain. At the next meeting, the complainers don't show up.

If paying dues discourages members from joining or staying in your club, drop the dues. Look for another way to make money for your club. For some hints on how to raise money for your club, read chapter 9, "Raising Money for Your Club."

Inventing your club handshake

A club handshake or salute is a special way to greet members at meetings or other times. You can also use the handshake to introduce new members and welcome them to the club.

When creating a handshake, use your imagination. Start with a standard handshake, then shake or lock fingertips only; link pinkies; press thumbs; rub palms, give the thumbs up; knock fists; or slap palms high, low, or to the side. Try adding other body parts as well, such as linking your arms or shaking your feet. For a crazy club body shake, jump up and down three times, turn in a circle, then fall to the floor and wriggle like an alligator. For a secret shake, think small: touch pinkies and wink or bump elbows when you pass another member.

Creating your code name

A code name is a special nickname you use when you're with other club members. Any type of club can use code names — they're for fun and make members feel close and united. Your code name may be a nickname you already use, or you can invent another one especially for the club.

Another option is to choose a code name based on the type of club you've organized. For example, in a basketball club, each member could choose a code name based on terms used in that sport, like Free Throw, Dribbler, Three Points, or Slam Dunk.

TRIVIA TIDBITS
White House Code Names

For security reasons, many U.S. government agencies use code names. Here are a few Secret Service code names of past Presidents and First Ladies:

- ◉ John F. Kennedy (Lancer)
- ◉ Jacqueline Kennedy (Lace)
- ◉ Ronald Reagan (Rawhide)
- ◉ Nancy Reagan (Rainbow)

Setting Up Your Club

To make your club run smoothly, it's important to set it up in a way that works for everyone. After the first meeting, you'll have an idea of how many members want to join, so you should be able to pick your club's structure. The structure you choose will depend on the type of club you have. A summer backyard club with four members might work better with one type of club. A school reading club might work better with another. To find the best structure for your club, answer the following questions:

- *Type:* Do you have a home or backyard club, a school club, or a place of worship or community center club?
- *Sponsor:* Do you have a sponsor who will be present at the meetings?
- *Number of members:* How many members will your club have?
- *Ages of members:* Are all the members the same age?

Skim the following descriptions of different club structures. Find the ones that most closely match your answers to the questions above, then read the descriptions more carefully and make your choice.

Once you've selected your club's structure, take note of the offices or duties that need to be filled. At the next meeting, describe the structure and decide when you'll choose or vote for officers or leaders. You'll find out how to do that in chapter 5.

A standard club

Type: Any type
Sponsor: Works with or without a sponsor
Number of members: From 3–4 to 10 or more
Ages of members: All the same age or around the same age

How it looks

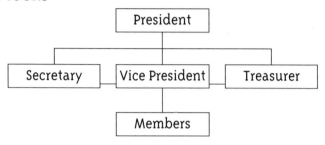

How it works

In a standard club, members elect four officers: president, vice president, secretary, and treasurer. The president is the leader, although all of the officers get an equal voice and vote. The other officers have special duties to perform in the club. The vice president assists the president, the treasurer keeps track of the money, and the secretary writes down what happens at each meeting.

Generally, this type of club has ten or more members so members outnumber officers. In a standard club with just three or four people, everyone is an officer. (If there are three people, the third person can be secretary and treasurer.)

A standard club works best when members are around the same age (within two or three years) because everyone has an equal chance to be elected for an office.

Officers can hold their offices for any length of time, but usually they stay in office for six months to a year. In an informal club in your backyard, home, place of worship, or community center, it might work better if officers are elected every month. That way, everyone has the opportunity to run for an office.

A club with other officers

Type: Any type
Sponsor: Not necessary
Number of members: From 5–8
Ages of members: Mixed or the same

How it looks

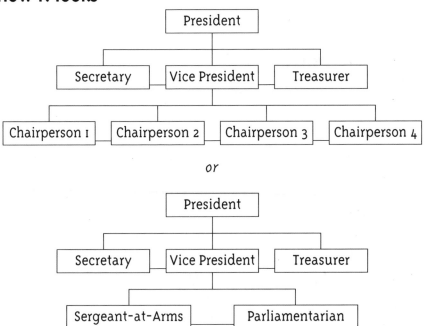

How it works

If you have a small club where all the members want to be officers, try this type of club. Often, members can choose a responsibility instead of holding an election and can rotate titles now and then.

In the first "How it looks" example, each member who is not an officer can take the title of chairperson. You can add chair positions as needed or name an assistant to each chairperson. You can have a meeting-activities chairperson (to plan games and other activities), a refreshment chairperson (to get refreshments for meetings), an atten-dance chairperson (to take roll and collect dues), or any other type of chairperson. Let members decide what activity they want to be involved in.

In the second "How It Looks" example, the offices of sergeant-at-arms and parliamentarian are added. The sergeant-at-arms keeps order and may call the meeting to order or swear in new members. The parliamentarian is an expert on the meeting rules (you'll learn more about these in chapter 7). This person can take roll or call for votes and tally the results.

A club without officers

Type: Home or backyard club; informal place of worship or community center club
Sponsor: Not necessary
Number of members: Small to medium group
Ages of members: Close to the same age

How it looks

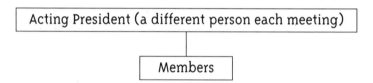

How it works

For an informal club where members generally get along, you might not need to elect officers. You'll still need someone to set up and run the meetings, but members can take turns at these tasks.

If you have members who are far apart in age (four or five years or more), try one of the other structures. In a club without officers, the older kids will generally want to lead, and very young kids might not be capable of organizing and running a meeting when it's their turn.

A club with historical titles

Type: Great for a home or backyard club; could be used in a school or community center club
Sponsor: Not necessary
Number of members: Any number
Ages of members: Mixed or the same

How it looks

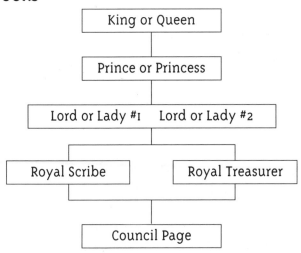

How it works

Clubs based on historical titles give a title and job to each member. The princess or prince is similar to a vice president, and the lords or ladies are similar to chairpersons. The royal scribe is the secretary, and the council page is a general errand runner.

If you need to, add more ladies and lords or use other historical titles, such as duchess, duke, baroness, baron, and knight.

Royalty Rules

- Kings were once elected but later usually inherited their crowns.
- A *monarchy* is ruled by one king or queen. A *dyarchy* is ruled by two kings.
- A *queen regent* is a woman who rules on her own.
- The wife of a king is called a *queen consort*.
- An unimportant prince is called a *princeling*.
- A *princess royal* is the eldest daughter of a king and queen.
- A prince's estate is called a *princedom*.

A "city government" club

Type: Any type; especially good for a school classroom club, student government club, or community center club
Sponsor: Works with or without a sponsor
Number of members: Any number
Ages of members: Mixed or the same

How it looks

How it works

A city government club is similar to the clubs with extra officers except that the mayor is mainly responsible for running the meetings. All members of the city council are equal. If the club is very large, you might have citizens who elect the mayor and council. The citizens can voice opinions at the meetings but don't vote on the decisions. If your club is small, you won't need citizens.

If all the club members get along well, this structure works because everyone has equal power, yet the mayor leads the meetings.

A "student council" club

Type: School club or large place of worship or community center club
Sponsor: Yes
Number of members: Large group
Ages of members: Usually mixed

How it looks

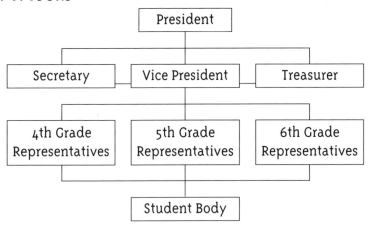

How it works

Like most governments or large associations, a student council is set up so a few people represent many others. The representatives ask people their wishes and opinions and then report these findings to the meeting. This club structure is for groups where not everyone could or would want to be involved in each meeting.

The officers may be nominated or picked to run (in some schools, representatives are chosen only from the oldest grades). In a place of worship or community center club, the officers and representatives could come from each grade or age group. All of the members (for example, the entire student body) elect the four main officers. Teachers or leaders may elect or assign the representatives, who bring information from the meetings to their homerooms or grade level.

Designing your own club

Over time, clubs change. Members quit and new ones join. Leaders may get tired of leading, and newer or younger members may want the opportunity to try.

For these and other reasons, you might find that your club will change structures to fit changing needs. You might also realize that none of these examples is exactly what you need. If this is the case, design a club structure that works for your group.

"We had a club with kids from three families that lasted for three or four years. We got along okay and didn't argue too much. It was fun. I think it worked because we had two main leaders in charge of the club who were also the oldest." —Josh

Choosing
Your Club's Officers

Officers are the leaders of the club. They are equal to the members when it comes time to vote, but they perform other duties as well. Does your club need officers? That depends on its type and structure. For example, if you have a student council club at school, a club with historical titles, or another type of formal club, you need officers. If you have an informal club, you don't need them. (Still, it's a good idea to review job checklists and duties in case you want to volunteer for a club job.)

Unless your club allows members to volunteer for offices, your members will need to vote for officers. Accepting an office sounds appealing, but keep in mind that it is also a job. Once you commit to an office, you should be prepared to come to all the meetings and stick with the job.

As you consider running or volunteering for an office, remember that certain people are better suited for a particular job than others. On pages 54–55 are descriptions of the four major offices, followed by a list of questions. Read the descriptions and answer the questions. The more positive responses you have, the better suited you are for the position.

Who does what?

President or club leader

The leader of the club is in charge of running and ending the meetings. The president or club leader is not the boss, but must be strong enough to have a final say about ending a discussion on an issue. He or she must be dedicated to the club and willing to spend extra time planning activities.

Is this job right for you? If you can answer "yes" to the following questions, you might consider running for club president or leader:

1. Can you make decisions easily?
2. Are you comfortable speaking in front of a group of people?
3. Can you hold your temper when others are disagreeing?
4. Can you encourage others to participate in activities without being bossy?

Vice president or second in charge

In a typical club setup, the vice president does the president's job when the president is absent. He or she may have other duties as well.

Is this job right for you? If you can answer "yes" to the following questions, you might consider running for club vice president or second in charge:

1. Will you feel okay about being second in charge instead of first?
2. Are you dependable?
3. Can you pick up new jobs and tasks quickly?
4. Can you speak comfortably in front of a group of people?

Treasurer

The treasurer takes care of the club money. He or she keeps it safe and knows exactly how much is there at all times. The treasurer must keep accurate records of money that comes in and goes out.

Is this job right for you? If you can answer "yes" to the following questions, you might consider running for club treasurer:

1. Are you good at math?
2. Are you organized?
3. Are you responsible and trustworthy?
4. Do you usually save some or all of your allowance and rarely have to borrow money?

"To be a good treasurer, the first thing you need to be is organized, but also good at math. You should be someone that the other members can trust." —Josh

Secretary

The secretary records in writing important notes and decisions made at club meetings. A secretary may also have other duties, such as tallying votes and handing out materials.

Some clubs may choose to combine the duties of secretary and treasurer. Still others may have a treasurer and eliminate the secretary's position.

Is this job right for you? If you can answer "yes" to the following questions, you might consider running for club secretary:

1. Do you write neatly and quickly?
2. Can you take notes well, picking out the important information from what is being said?
3. Do you read well aloud?
4. Can you expect to attend all the meetings?

"I belong to the safety patrol club at school. We meet every morning and also once a month to talk about problems and promotions. All kids start out as a trainee, working with someone else to learn. Then you get a white badge. Next you're promoted to sergeant, then lieutenant, and then captain. You also have to keep up your grades — A's and B's, and only two C's are allowed each year. I'm a lieutenant, and I might be able to make captain this year. I consider myself a leader because I can be strict and nice, too. I believe that good leaders should always do their best." —Miles

Electing the officers

There are several ways to decide who will lead your club. If you wish to vote for officers, you'll need a list of members who want to run for each office. These members are the candidates. In a formal club, such as a student council, members nominate or suggest candidates for each office. In an informal club, members can either be nominated by other members or sign up to run.

Campaigning

You've probably seen campaign ads for candidates running for city, county, state, or national offices. Before each election, their ads and speeches bombard the TV, mail, and newspapers. In a school, candidates for student council usually campaign as well. In the weeks before the election, they might hang posters and hand out cards, flyers, or small items with their name and the office they're seeking. They might make speeches at school assemblies.

In most clubs, the process of selecting officers isn't as showy and doesn't go on as long. In fact, once members have selected nominees and recorded their names, they can vote for their choice. If the decision can't be made that easily, club members might ask the nominees to stand and tell why they would like the office and what ideas they plan to bring to the club.

Giving a short speech can be difficult for anyone who is not prepared, so if club members decide to require a speech, it's a good idea to announce the positions that are open at one meeting and then vote on them at the next meeting. This gives the candidates time to collect their thoughts and make certain they really want to try for the job or office.

If you're thinking about running for an office, look again at the qualifications for that office and how you match up. Use the qualifications to plan your speech. As you compose your speech, be careful to make promises you can really keep. If you tell the club that, as president, you'll buy them a two-story clubhouse, you'd better have the money to back up your promise.

CLUB FLUB!

You're running for club president, and the members have asked you to give a campaign speech. You start out with "Ummm...." and "I think it would be neat if...," call the other candidates "losers" and "jerks," and end with a mumbled "Well, that's about it."

When you're preparing your campaign, remember K.I.S.S. — Keep It Short and Simple. Think of one or two qualifications for the office and tell how you best fulfill them. Then think of one or two ideas you have to help the club and describe them. Wrap up your speech by asking the group to vote for you. You don't even need to mention the other candidates, and you definitely shouldn't say bad things about them.

Voting

After the candidates give their speeches, it's time to vote. When you're deciding which candidate to vote for, keep the interests of your club in mind. Vote for the person you believe can do the best job — even if that person isn't you or your best friend.

When you vote for officers, use the secret official ballot (see the following page). You can either read the nominees' names out loud and have members write down their choice on a slip of paper, or you can make ballots.

A ballot lists each office and the nominees. Members cast their ballots by choosing the people they want and placing their completed ballots in a ballot box. You can make ballots on a computer and print them out, or write them by hand on slips of paper. If you have many members, ask your sponsor or another adult to photocopy enough ballots for everyone.

You'll need a ballot box or container to hold the completed ballots. A shoe box with a lid makes a good ballot box. On the lid, cut a slit that is about 1/2" wide and 4" long. Ask voters to fold their ballots in half and slip them into the box. Wait until all the ballots have been cast before you tally them.

If possible, have someone who is not a candidate count the votes — better yet, have two people read and tally the votes to make sure the voting is accurate. Count the total votes twice. Both people must arrive at the same total.

Also make sure that the total number of votes for each office is the same as your total membership number. If you have more votes than members, then someone voted twice. If this happens, the election isn't valid and will have to be redone. Never tell how many votes any individual received.

How to Make a Secret Official Ballot

1. Cut a sheet of plain white paper into halves or thirds, depending on how many offices and candidates you have.

2. At the top of the ballot, write "Official Ballot." Include directions to check only one name in each category.

3. Write the title of each position across the top of the ballot, under the directions.

4. Under each title, list the full names (first and last) of the nominees in alphabetical order (this way you won't be playing favorites by putting one person's name first).

5. Beside each name, draw a box. Make it large enough so voters can place a check or "X" in it.

OFFICIAL BALLOT

Vote for *one* candidate for each title. To cast your vote, put a check mark or "X" in the box beside the candidate's name.

Offices and Candidates

President		**Vice President**	
Christy Allen	❐	Wil Haung	❐
Trent Davidson	❐	Risa Mathews	❐
Andy Garcia	❐		

Treasurer		**Secretary**	
Jessica Able	❐	Joy Baker	❐
Quinten Brooks	❐	Phan Lo	❐
Raul Diaz	❐		
Cinda Smith	❐		

Winning and losing gracefully

If you win an election, smile and say "Thank you" to the other members. Be polite to the candidates who didn't win. This shows maturity and good manners.

If you lose an election, this doesn't mean that nobody likes you. It simply means that more people voted for another candidate than voted for you. Even if you feel that the winner isn't as qualified for the office as you are, keep these feelings to yourself. Offer to help the winner in whatever way you can. You can run for office again at a later date.

CLUB FLUB!

The members cast their ballots and tallied the votes. When they announced the winners, your name wasn't called. You storm out of the room, vowing never to run for an office again.

If you lose an election, you'll probably feel disappointed. That's only natural. Try not to let the loss affect your attitude about the club and the other members. Prove that you're good leadership material by shaking the winner's hand and congratulating him or her. Keep going to meetings and participating in the activities and votes. Focus on having an enjoyable club experience. There really will be a "next time."

Creating Your
Club Headquarters

Clubs need a place to meet, work, and socialize. Home and back-yard clubs might meet in a tree house or a member's basement or recreation room. A school club will probably meet in a classroom, cafeteria, gym, or other area of the school. Places of worship and community centers often have meeting rooms or recreation areas that you might be able to use. A sports club might meet at the skating rink, gym, or playing field.

Borrow a space

Where should your club meet? If it's just getting started, consider borrowing a space until your club gets going. Look for a space you can temporarily call your headquarters.

Inside space

Meeting inside is comfortable — you're usually out of the heat, cold, or rain — and there are probably chairs or other places to sit. There might even be places to work on projects and store supplies.

For home clubs, ask your parents if you can use part of the living room, basement, finished attic, or your bedroom. If each member wants a chance to host a meeting, take turns meeting at a different home each time. For added privacy inside, make a tent with blankets or sheets. You can also stake out an area with chairs or pile up pillows and cushions in a circle. If you live in an apartment complex and have a recreation room, check with the manager about meeting there.

Where you meet at school, in a place of worship, or at a community center will be up to the principal, teacher, or youth director. If you have an idea of where to meet, make a suggestion but be flexible. Schools in particular are often crowded with before- and after-school care for kids as well as other club and faculty meetings. You may have to meet in a different room every time, share the cafeteria with other groups, or meet on the school stage with the curtain closed.

Outside space

Outside, you can find dozens of club spaces if you use your imagination. If meeting space is hard to come by at your school, place of worship, or community center, ask to meet under a covered walkway, breezeway, or on the lawn. For home clubs, any corner or side yard will do for a meeting place — sidewalks and garages are also possibilities. Many apartment complexes have outdoor spaces including stairwells, landings, courtyards, and carports. If you live near a wooded lot, look for a clearing where you can hold neighborhood club meetings. Trees are a natural club hangout. Set up underneath one or climb up and assign branches (but be careful!).

Use items in your yard or driveway to make a club space for a home or backyard club. Meet under a trampoline, behind a storage shed, or next to a large bush. A tent is the perfect clubhouse because it's private, you can move it, and it's already built. If you have two small tents, put them together so the openings face each other for a duplex clubhouse.

TRIVIA TIDBITS

Ancient Meeting Places

- In Latin, *forum* means *open space*. In ancient Roman towns, the forum was the place where people met for business or to conduct city government.
- In ancient Greece, people used a public area, called an *agora,* for city meetings.
- In both ancient Rome and Greece, people exercised in large gymnasiums, but they also used the gyms as meeting places for social groups and businesses.

Build your own clubhouse

With imagination and a few tools, you can turn ordinary supplies into your own clubhouse. Building a clubhouse is a great project for a home or backyard club, or one that meets at a recreation center or is part of an after-school program. You don't always need a large space for a clubhouse. Sometimes a corner, inside or outside, is enough.

Safety first

You might use a variety of tools to build your clubhouse — but be sure to remember that all tools, including power tools, can be dangerous if you don't know the proper way to use them or if you use them for the wrong purpose. Carpentry tools for woodworking can be especially dangerous, so get an adult to help you practice with them before you try by yourself. Once you know how to use tools, respect them and use them as they were intended.

Building materials

Ropes and fabric

Ropes and fabric are handy building materials that you probably already have around your home. You can combine the two to make a wall inside or out. In addition to rope and a sheet of fabric (for example, an old bedsheet, a blanket, or a drop cloth), you'll need several large safety pins or clothespins.

Tie the rope between two trees, poles, or other secured objects. Drape the fabric over the rope. Secure the fabric with the safety pins or clothespins. If you want to make a triangular tent room, use two sheets (one for each side).

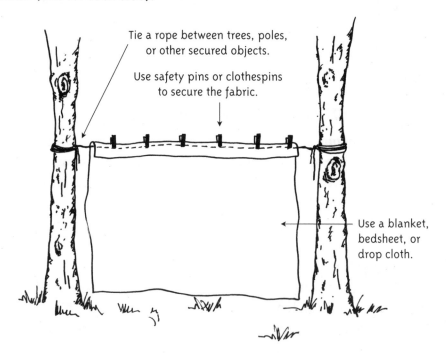

Tie a rope between trees, poles, or other secured objects.

Use safety pins or clothespins to secure the fabric.

Use a blanket, bedsheet, or drop cloth.

You can also convert existing outdoor objects — such as swing sets and picnic tables — into a private space using fabric. You'll need a sheet of fabric and some rope. Tie the fabric onto each wide side of a swing set. Pull the swings out of the way and sit on the ground, or use the swings as seats. To make a club area out of a picnic table, drape one or two sheets of fabric over the sides, anchoring the fabric on top of the table with a heavy flower pot, books, or other objects. Save fabric scraps or old towels to make coverings for windows or doors.

Boxes

Cardboard boxes are the ideal building material for your headquarters because they're lightweight, easy to cut and shape, and free. Look for cardboard boxes at the curb or trash dumpster on garbage pickup days. Large appliance boxes for refrigerators or stoves are the best. If you can't find any discarded ones, look in the phone book and call a local appliance store. Ask them if you can have their discarded boxes. Many supermarkets will provide cardboard boxes at no cost.

Use scissors to cut the boxes, and duct tape or other sturdy tape to hold them together. If scissors won't cut through the thick cardboard, ask a parent or sponsor to help by using a utility knife. Utility knives are sharp and difficult to control, so get help when using one.

To make a shutter window or a door that opens and closes, draw the size and shape you want on the box. For a shutter window, draw a rectangle and divide it in half vertically to create the shutters. Cut on the lines except on the two outside edges, which will be folds. Open and bend the shutters back and forth. You may need to trim around them so they open without sticking.

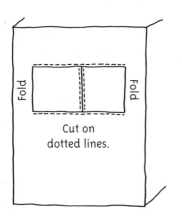

Fold

Fold

Cut on
dotted lines.

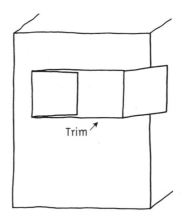

Trim

For a door, draw a rectangle at the bottom of the box. Cut the top, bottom, and one of the sides (the other side will be the fold). You can decorate your boxes with almost any type of paint, markers, stickers, or crayons.

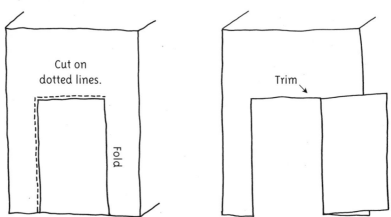

Fasteners and tools

Scissors, twine, wire, tape, safety pins, and glue can all be used to fasten paper or cloth. Push pins (which are like thumbtacks only longer) are especially handy. They are easier to push in and remove and hold better than thumbtacks. Use push pins to secure fabric or paper to wood.

Staple guns

A staple gun can be used to attach fabric or cardboard to boards or other objects. Staple guns come in different sizes and require different amounts of effort to make the staples penetrate the surface. A lightweight one might work better for you since heavy-duty ones are more difficult to use. (Find a pair of clear safety goggles to wear for protection.) Always have an adult supervise when you use a staple gun, never point one at another person, and watch your fingers!

Hammers

The most common hammer is a claw hammer, which is metal and has a claw-like device on one end to pull out nails. To start a nail, hold it in position with your free hand and tap it a few times until it stands on its own. Hold the hammer near the end of its handle, gently tapping it on the nail. If you bend the nail, use the claw end to remove it, and start over with a new nail in a new place.

When hammering, wear clear safety goggles to protect your eyes from flying nails. Remember to keep nails out of the grass where someone might step on one. Store nails by size in jars or coffee cans.

Saws

If you need to shorten a board, use a crosscut saw, which cuts straight lines across the grain of a board. All saws are sharp and dangerous. If they can cut wood, they can also cut your fingers, so get training first and always use one with an adult around to supervise.

Before you pick up the saw, use a pencil and ruler to mark the wood where you want to cut. Then set the board on a table, sawhorse, or other sturdy surface; support the weight of the other end with your hand. If the board is especially long, have someone hold the board down or sit on it. Run the saw slowly back and forth over the pencil mark. Continue to move the saw back and forth smoothly. If the saw is sharpened, it shouldn't be too hard to cut off the excess wood.

CLUB FLUB!

Your club is building its first tree house and everyone's brought tools. Suddenly it begins to rain. In the scramble to get indoors, you leave your dad's favorite hammer outside.

When your club decides to build a clubhouse, first decide who will bring what. How many hammers, nails, and other tools will you need? Get permission to borrow tools. Will you need help from an adult? Store tools safely in a toolbox or shoe box when you're not using them.

"We built our clubhouse in the corner of the field behind our house. The clubhouse had a tunnel and a guard that you had to tell a password to. We painted the clubhouse green, brown, and black like camouflage and painted on our names, squiggly lines, and peace signs." —John Michael

Designs to try

In this section, you'll find a few clubhouse designs you might want to try. Any of these ideas could be used by a home or backyard club.

Soft lean-to

Materials: Fence or wall; one or two bedsheets or large pieces of plastic; push pins, staple gun, or a hammer and nails; bricks, potted plants, or other heavy objects; 2 1/2- or 3-foot pole or stick (optional).

Secure the top side of the sheet or plastic to the top of a fence, using the push pins, staple gun, or hammer and nails. Stretch the sheet out at an angle; use the heavy objects to anchor it to the ground. If the sheet sags in the middle, push the pole or stick into the ground under the sheet to prop it up.

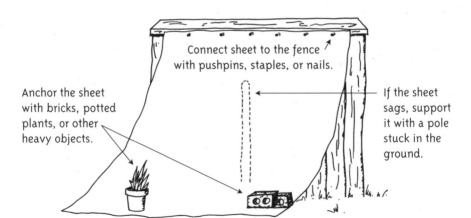

Connect sheet to the fence with pushpins, staples, or nails.

Anchor the sheet with bricks, potted plants, or other heavy objects.

If the sheet sags, support it with a pole stuck in the ground.

Canopy

Materials: Bedsheet or lightweight blanket; four posts or sturdy branches with one end sharpened on each (have your sponsor or another adult help you sharpen them with a knife); yarn or string; scissors.

A canopy is nice on warm days when you want some shade. Lay the bedsheet on the ground, and at each of the four corners, cut a small hole. Next, position the posts at each corner of the sheet. Remove the sheet and force the sharp ends of the posts into the ground. Loop the string or yarn in each hole, then tie the sheet to the top of the posts at the corners.

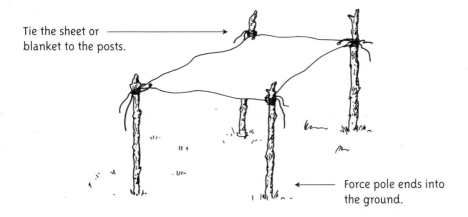

Tie the sheet or blanket to the posts.

Force pole ends into the ground.

Wilderness lean-to

Materials: Nine long branches (the longer the better; cut off any twigs) or poles; eight smaller branches, with one end sharpened (cut off any twigs); rope; leafy branches, palm fronds, bedsheets, blankets, or plastic.

If you live in a wooded area, you can use fallen limbs and branches to make a wilderness lean-to. This hideaway takes a little time to make, but it's worth the effort. You can also make this lean-to in a yard using wooden or aluminum poles.

Find two trees that stand side by side about 10 feet apart. If they have forks at about the same height, that's even better. Place one of the long branches across from fork to fork; secure it to the tree with a rope; this is your cross branch. Lean two long branches on either end of the cross branch; these are your supports. Check the height and amount of lean. If the cross branch is too high in the tree and the lean is too vertical, you won't have room for many club members underneath. If the cross branch is too low and the lean is flat, you won't have room to sit up.

Adjust the two supports (you might want to secure them to the cross branch with rope). Add two more long branches to the cross branch, spaced evenly apart.

Space the eight smaller branches or poles on the outside of the frame, four on each side. These will hold up the cross supports, which you'll add later. Drive the branches into the ground. If the soil is hard, bring a shovel to help dig the little holes.

Once the branches are set, lay the remaining four long branches (or cross supports) across the eight little branches. (Secure them with rope, if you want.) Cover the lean-to with leafy branches, palm fronds, or sheets of fabric.

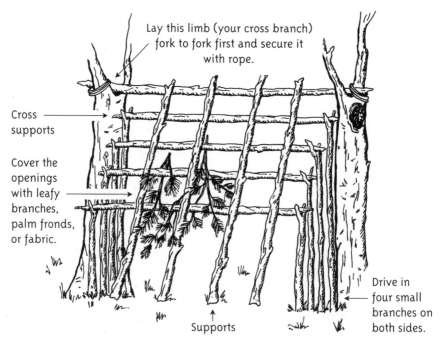

Lay this limb (your cross branch) fork to fork first and secure it with rope.

Cross supports

Cover the openings with leafy branches, palm fronds, or fabric.

Drive in four small branches on both sides.

Supports

"There was a little field our club would go to that had lots of hay. We would put plastic bags over our hands to keep them from itching and gather the hay. Then we would make big nests to sit in. The man who mowed was nice enough not to mow down our nests." —Stephanie

Double box clubhouse

Materials: Two large appliance boxes (about the same size); duct tape; scissors.

Cut off the flaps at the top of the box. Cut downward along the same corner of each box. Open up each box at the cut. One side of each box will now have an extra panel.

Turn the two boxes so they open to each other, and cut a door and any windows you want. Then slide the boxes together, overlap the sides, and tape along the seams. Tape the corners on the floor flaps to make the double box clubhouse stronger. Leave the roof open or drape fabric over it.

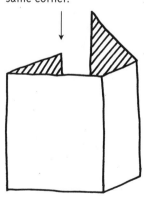

Cut both boxes down the same corner.

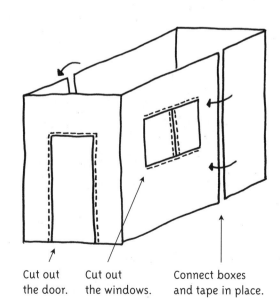

Cut out the door.   Cut out the windows.   Connect boxes and tape in place.

Hinged box hideaway

Materials: Large cardboard boxes; duct tape; scissors.

Cut off the top flaps from several large cardboard boxes. Connect them with pieces of duct tape (about two or three pieces, spaced evenly between the panels). Use your "hideaway" to corral off a corner of the yard, or shape it into a circle or zigzag. This hideaway is portable, so you can take it to another member's home and fold it away after each meeting.

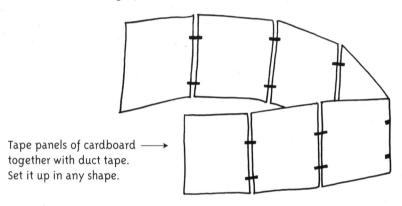

Tape panels of cardboard ⟶
together with duct tape.
Set it up in any shape.

Scavengers' clubhouse

Materials: Anything and everything, including boards, lattice panels, tires, metal, and fabric.

This is a clubhouse built of materials and objects you have available — it'll look different for each club, depending on what you can find. This clubhouse is semi-permanent, so get permission before building it in the backyard or anywhere else.

Look for a solid object to act as one clubhouse wall, such as a fence, tree, or shed. Next, gather discarded junk from a garage or trash pile (ask your sponsor or another adult to supervise). Be careful when foraging through used supplies. Hammer down nails that stick out or remove them. Watch for sharp metal edges and wire that could cut you, and be sure to wear a pair of work gloves to protect your hands.

Get club members together and brainstorm how to use the found items. Use an old plastic wading pool as a roof or the club spa. Lean a large board against a wall or fence for a crawl-in lean-to. Narrower boards make good walkways, gangways, and ramps — make sure the boards are sturdy and supported well before walking on them.

Use old lawn chairs or bucket seats from cars for club chairs. Make tables out of wooden crates or large empty pails. If you're **lucky**, perhaps you'll find assembled cabinets, shelves, and sheets of **panel**ing for walls.

Use several large, old tires placed side by side so their openings form a "tunnel." Dig a shallow trench the width of the row of tires. Anchor the tunnel in place by filling the open space at the bottom of each tire with dirt and pebbles. Pack it down firmly.

To make a table, balance a piece of wood on top of several tires. A tire swing is a welcome addition to any club built around a large tree.

"The best clubhouses we have made are ones that we all worked together on, used what we could find, and made them up along the way." —Mark

7

Running the Meetings

During meetings, members plan and make decisions. Although club members might work on projects at other times, meetings are still needed to discuss progress and problems.

Your club will need to decide how often you want to meet. A home or backyard club might meet as often as twice a week, with members also working on club projects on their own time. Other clubs only hold meetings once a week or once a month. It's up to you!

Try to pick a meeting time and place that's convenient for all members or have members vote on where and when they'd like to meet.

Informal meetings

Every club has informal meetings at times, and some club types (such as a home, backyard, or community center club) may choose this style of meeting for every session. At informal meetings, members gather either for fun or to work together on a project.

Even though these meetings are relaxed, they should have a goal or purpose. To start the meeting, the club leader can welcome everyone and announce or remind members of the meeting's purpose. He or she can end the meeting by stopping activities and reminding everyone of upcoming events or the next meeting time.

Formal meetings

Often, clubs run more smoothly when the meetings follow a certain order every time. Keeping the meeting format the same is especially important in clubs with many members. Clubs with formal meetings can run the first part of their meetings using *parliamentary procedure*. The second part can include fun activities such as games, refreshments, or working on a project.

Parliamentary procedure

Parliamentary procedure — a set of steps used to run a meeting — was first used in Great Britain's House of Parliament. Following are the basic steps needed to run a formal meeting using parliamentary procedure.

Step 1: Call to order

The president or club leader begins the meeting by saying, "This meeting is called to order." He or she may bang a gavel (a wooden hammer) or make a knocking sound on the table or floor to get everyone's attention. Members should stop talking and listen.

Step 2: Secretary's report

The president asks the secretary to read the minutes or notes from the last meeting. The secretary stands and reads the minutes. (For more about minutes, see pages 78–79.)

Step 3: Treasurer's report

After the minutes, the president asks the treasurer to give the treasurer's report. The treasurer stands and does this. If your club collects regular dues, the treasurer collects them now. (For more about the treasurer's report, see page 79.)

Step 4: Old business

The president asks members if there's any old business to discuss. Old business includes projects your club has been working on since the last meeting or problems that you weren't able to solve at that time.

Members raise their hands to speak, and the president calls their names one at a time. Everyone should get a chance to talk without interruptions. If an argument begins, the president should step in, call the meeting back to order, then ask the members to vote on how to resolve the disagreement.

Step 5: New business

The club president calls for new business, ideas for the future, and conversation about upcoming events. Members can also make announcements or share news and updates about projects at this time. Just as in step 4, the president should call for a vote if any disagreements arise.

The last piece of new business should include setting the agenda, or plans, for the next meeting. That way, members will know what to expect. Be sure to include something fun (see chapter 8 for ideas).

Step 6: Adjournment

When the talking is over and your meeting time is up, the president ends the meeting by saying, "This meeting is adjourned."

Motions and seconds

Many clubs will be able to run their meetings smoothly by using just the six steps described above. If you want an even more structured meeting, you can also use motions and seconds. A *motion* is a request that starts with the phrase "I move that." A *second* is a response that leads to a discussion of the motion.

Here's how it works: Let's say a youth group is trying to decide how to entertain a group of younger children. One member says, "I move that we put on a skit." Another member backs up the motion by saying, "I second the motion," or simply, "Second." The president calls for discussion of the idea. When everyone who wants to express an opinion has had the chance, the president calls for a vote.

The president may call for a motion anytime during the meeting. If everyone has been discussing something but no one has moved to approve an idea, the president would ask, "Is there a motion to put on a skit?" Then he or she would ask for a second. If no one seconds a motion, it usually means that the rest of the group is not interested in the idea, and it's time to move on. Don't be offended if your ideas aren't always seconded. There will be other opportunities for you to put your ideas into action.

In a club that uses motions and seconds, the leader ends all meetings by asking for a motion and second to adjourn the meeting.

"I had a club with three other girls. We met at my friend Nancy's house. Before we started our meetings, we would hold hands and say that we would always be friends. We liked to use parliamentary procedure during our meetings. That was part of the fun. We even used motions and seconds.

"Nancy led the meetings because it was her house. She had a gavel she got from somewhere, and she would hit it on the table and call the meeting to order. We took turns taking the minutes of the meeting." —Jan

The minutes of the meeting

In club language, minutes are the official records of the meeting. Formal meetings generally use minutes to keep track of who made motions, what decisions members made, and what tasks members volunteered to do. Informal clubs don't need to keep minutes, but it still may be worthwhile and fun to try. If your club members tend to argue about what happened at the last meeting or about who said they would help out on which project, minutes can help. When what happened is written down, it's more difficult to disagree.

Even though this record is called minutes, the secretary shouldn't try to record every minute of the meeting. Keeping good minutes is like taking good notes in class — you only need to write down the important or key ideas.

Club secretaries can create and practice their own shorthand, or abbreviated writing, to make the task easier. Here are some examples of words that might commonly be in the minutes and how they can be abbreviated:

- ⊚ president — pres.
- ⊚ vice president — v.p.
- ⊚ secretary — sec.
- ⊚ treasurer — treas.
- ⊚ member — mem.
- ⊚ and — &
- ⊚ about — ab.
- ⊚ motion — mot.
- ⊚ second — 2nd
- ⊚ vote — vt.

The secretary should always include the date of the meeting at the beginning of the minutes and keep the minutes together in a notebook.

The treasurer's report

The treasurer should have a notebook to record money that has been put into and taken out of the club's treasury. At each meeting, the treasurer will announce how much money the club has at that point in time. He or she can also announce how much money the club spent since the last meeting, how much the club earned from a fundraiser, and how close the club is to reaching a specific goal — for example, having enough money to buy club T-shirts for all members.

"When I was treasurer of our club, at the end of each meeting I would total our club money, then have someone else check it in case I made a mistake." —William

CLUB FLUB!

You're the club treasurer. At the beginning of a meeting, two new members arrive and give you their dues, which you stuff into your pocket. Then the refreshment chairperson asks you for money to cover her costs; you search your backpack for the club money. When the meeting starts, the president asks how much money the club has. You reach into your pocket and then your backpack, pull out some coins and crumpled bills, and begin counting.

If you're the treasurer, find one place to keep the club money — that way it'll be ready when you or the other club members need it. You can keep the money in any kind of container (a shoe box, piggy bank, a box with a lock, etc.), or you can open a bank account for storing larger amounts of money. Your sponsor or another adult can help you open the new account.

Keep track of all the money in a notebook and write down the exact amounts taken out of or put into the treasury. For each time, include the date and an explanation of where the money came from or where it was spent. You should always know how much is in the treasury when it's time for the treasurer's report.

Example of Treasurer's Entries

June 14

Starting Amount in Treasury:
   $6.45

Jamal put in $3.50 — club
   fundraiser

Janice put in $0.25 — club dues

Total $10.20

June 21

Starting Amount in Treasury:
   $10.20

Tan took out $5.00 — club
   refreshments

Total $5.20

Keeping Meetings Fun and Interesting

How do you keep club members interested and meetings fun? You might start each meeting with an activity. Or take a break in the middle to stretch, laugh, and relax. You might unwind at the end and treat yourselves to some refreshments. In this chapter, you'll learn about lots of ways to make your meetings enjoyable for everyone.

Choosing a mascot

A mascot is a person, animal, or thing that represents your club. Students often use an image of an eagle or bear to represent their school because these animals symbolize pride, courage, or strength. For your club, you might choose a pet or stuffed animal for your mascot. You can use your mascot in your emblem and in other projects.

"My friends and I had a club. We called ourselves 'The Butterflies.' My dog was our mascot. We bought T-shirts and wrote our name on them. We made one for my dog, too." —Sarah

Club stuff to make

A club emblem

An emblem is a drawing or design that represents your club. Businesses use logos — emblems with slogans — to sell their products. Video, shoe, food, and toy companies all use logos, and you can probably recognize several without even looking at the company's name. Usually a logo or emblem communicates something about the company or its products; your emblem can do the same for your club. A dirt bike club might use a bike in its emblem; a detective club might use a magnifying glass; and a fitness club might use barbells.

What if each member has an idea for the emblem? Have an emblem contest. Ask members to draw their ideas. Post the designs without names and ask members to vote on which one they like best.

CLUB FLUB!

The club picks you to design their new emblem. You spend a whole week creating it on your computer with the latest and greatest drawing programs. The trouble is, it's too complicated!

When designing an emblem, think about how it'll be used. Will it be large so it can be put on a flag or banner, or smaller to fit on a T-shirt? No matter how your club will use the emblem, keep it simple. Basic shapes — stripes, circles, and triangles — work well, as do simple line drawings with no shading.

A club flag or banner

You can hang a club flag or banner on the wall where you meet or on the outside of a clubhouse. The difference between a flag and banner is the shape and how it's hung. A flag is rectangular and hangs from a pole; a banner is long and thin or any crazy shape you like. You can drape a banner across a wall or table or hang it from the ceiling.

You don't need much to create a flag or banner — a scrap of fabric or an old pillowcase works well. You'll also need fabric markers, permanent markers, or fabric paint; glue; a piece of cardboard; scissors; and a stick, pole, or broomstick.

Use the markers or paint to decorate the fabric or pillowcase. Copy your emblem on your flag or banner, if you have one, and add your club name.

If you're using a pillowcase, you can stop the design from bleeding through to the other side by slipping the piece of cardboard into the opening before painting. Let one side dry overnight before decorating the other side. Once you've decorated the pillowcase, close the opening and glue it shut. Squeeze a double line of glue near the edge, and spread the glue with your fingers. Press the sides together and let dry.

As you glue the pillowcase shut, notice the turned-down hem, which is about 3 inches wide. You'll slip the flag's pole into this hem. Slit the casing at the bottom of your flag. Insert the stick, pole, or broomstick into the hole and push it gently through the casing. Don't open the casing at the top.

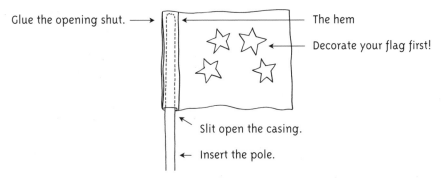

Glue the opening shut. ⟶   The hem

Decorate your flag first!

Slit open the casing.

← Insert the pole.

You can make a banner from either a long strip of poster paper or fabric. If the banner fabric is cotton, you might want to finish the edges to keep them from raveling. To do this, fold over the edges and glue them down. Decorate one side and tack your banner to a wall.

TRIVIA TIDBITS
Fun Flag Facts

- The largest flag in regular use is in Brazil; it measures more than 200 feet by 300 feet.
- *Vexillology* is the study of flags; that word comes from the Latin word *vexillum,* which means *flag.*
- The American Stars and Stripes flag has been changed 27 times since it was officially adopted in 1777.
- Flags were once made of silk or linen. Today they're made of less expensive materials such as cotton, nylon, and polyester.

Club T-shirts

Choral groups, sports teams, cheerleading and dance squads, Boy Scouts and Girl Scouts of America, and Camp Fire Kids are just a few clubs that wear uniforms or matching clothing. Why not make matching T-shirts for your club?

Clubs in a school or place of worship often can raise enough money to buy printed T-shirts or sweatshirts. If your club has raised enough money, your sponsor or another adult can help you place the T-shirt order.

Even if your club can't raise enough money, you can still have a club T-shirt. You can buy multi-packs of white T-shirts or use old T-shirts or sweatshirts you already have. If the shirts have writing on them, turn them inside out and cut off the tags. Use permanent markers or fabric paints to decorate your shirts. Don't forget to add your club name.

How to Letter a T-Shirt

When you're lettering your T-shirt — or even a banner or flag — plan ahead and use the following instructions to center and space your lettering. You'll need shirts, a piece of lined paper, a pencil, a ruler, and fabric markers or paint.

1. Write the name of your club on the piece of paper.

2. Count how many letters and spaces are in the name, and then find the middle letter of the name. For example: *4th Street Club* has fifteen letters and spaces. The middle letter is the first *e* in the word *Street* because there are seven letters and spaces on each side.

3. Use a ruler to measure across your shirt. Divide the width in half to find the center of your shirt. Or you can fold the shirt in half and mark the center where the fold is.

4. Print or write the middle letter on the middle of the shirt.

5. Working from the middle, print or write the letters. You can start working in either the right or left direction. Use one finger to space between each letter; use two fingers to space between each word. At first it'll seem strange to write the beginning of your club name in right to left order, but as long as you check your spelling and spacing, it'll work out fine.

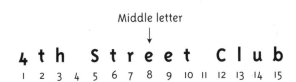

Middle letter
↓

4 t h   S t r e e t   C l u b
1 2 3   4 5 6 7 8 9 10 11 12 13 14 15

Club ID cards

Identification cards are an easy project that takes only one meeting to make. You'll need a library card or expired credit card to use as a guide; poster board or other stiff paper; a pencil; scissors; an ink pad or marker; school photos; and clear adhesive-backed shelf paper.

Trace the library card or credit card on the poster board or stiff paper and cut out one card for each member. On one side of your card, write your name and the name of the club. You can also add the date you joined the club. On the other side of your card, make an I.D. print by rolling your thumb on the ink pad and then pressing your thumb down onto the card. (If you don't have an ink pad, you can use a marker. Draw on the pad of one thumb and press the thumb on your I.D. card.) Glue a small school photo next to your I.D. print.

To make your card last longer, sandwich it between two pieces of the clear shelf paper and press down. Press out any wrinkles and bubbles. Trim around the card.

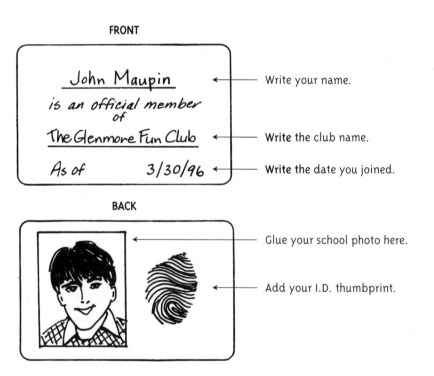

FRONT

John Maupin ← Write your name.

is an official member of

The Glenmore Fun Club ← Write the club name.

As of 3/30/96 ← Write the date you joined.

BACK

← Glue your school photo here.

← Add your I.D. thumbprint.

Club stickers

The great thing about making stickers is that you can pull out this activity whenever the mood strikes you. You'll need permanent markers; a roll of white shelf paper from a discount, hardware, or grocery store (adhesive-backed); and scissors.

On the shelf paper, trace around objects such as cups and small boxes for a guide, or try any shapes you want. Decorate the shapes with your club name and emblem and cut out your stickers.

Games with a purpose

Most club members like to play games, and they're a good way to relax in the middle of a meeting or have fun together at the end. The following games are more than fun — they build teamwork, trust, and imagination.

Building teamwork

Teamwork and cooperation are essential to keeping a club together. When everyone works toward the same goal, you can reach that goal faster and more easily.

Human knot

You can play this game at the first meeting or anytime you want. Use a stopwatch and try to untie yourselves faster each time you play. This game works best with five or more players — the more, the better.

Directions: Stand in a circle facing in. Stretch out your arms and grab hands with two different people across from you. Don't hold hands with the people next to you. You may have to reach over or around others to find an empty hand.

Now try to untie the knot without dropping hands. You'll have to talk about options, take turns, and step over and around people, but don't let go. If someone drops hands, just start over.

Club juggling

Try this game to work on group cooperation and coordination. You'll need several soft objects, such as sponge balls, tennis balls, or rolled-up socks.

Directions: Stand in a circle facing toward the center. One person begins by tossing the ball (or other object) to another person, that person tosses the ball to another, and so on until everyone has thrown and caught the ball and the ball is back to the first person. Don't pass the ball around in a circle, work back and forth across the circle instead. Remember who passed the ball to you and who you tossed it to.

Start the sequence again. Once you've started, the first person tosses in a second ball and begins the second sequence while the first is still going. See how long you can keep the balls moving without messing up the sequence. When the group has mastered two balls, add another, and another. The goal is to be able to keep as many balls going as there are players.

Building trust

A strong club depends on your commitment to each other as members. When you trust and rely on each other, your club will be united.

Blindfold walk

Can you trust your fellow club members to guide you through an obstacle course? You'll need blindfolds and a room with furniture you can rearrange or a large yard with obstacles such as lawn chairs, garbage cans, and toys.

Directions: Count off and team up in pairs. Try to change pairs each time the game is played. Blindfold one person from each pair. The other person in the pair acts as the blindfolded person's guide. If you're inside, rearrange the furniture. If you're outside, set up the obstacles.

Have pairs line up on one side of the room or yard. Each pair's goal is to cross to the other side as quickly as possible without running into anything. Guides must talk their blindfolded partners across the room without touching them. The blindfolded partners must not touch anything either and must only use the cues and suggestions their partners give. Since several pairs will be talking at once, concentration and trust are important.

Free fall
Put yourself in the hands of your fellow members. This game is best played by members who are close to the same size.

Directions: Members line up in two lines facing each other, arms outstretched. One person stands at the head of the line with his or her back turned to the others. This person keeps a stiff body and drops into the arms of the members. The catching group should keep their legs slightly bent and be prepared to give a little when they catch the falling person. Make sure there are at least three people on each side of the line to act as catchers.

Building imagination
Imagination is important to your club — with imagination you can brainstorm ideas for names, projects, or anything you wish.

Imagination challenge
Spark your creativity and imagination with this game, which challenges you to picture familiar people as something other than human.

Directions: One player leaves the room or goes someplace where he or she can't hear the group. Together, the remaining members think of a person — either a club member, classmate, friend, family member, or teacher — that everyone knows.

Once the members have thought of a person, the member who was gone can return. The returning member has to guess the person the other members are thinking of.

First, the group tells whether the person is a member or not. Then the guesser asks five different people a question about the mystery person. Each question, however, must begin with the phrase "If the person were a ..." and end with the phrase "... what would he or she be?"

For example, the guesser could ask, "If the person were a color, what would he or she be?" The guesser could ask what the mystery person would be if he or she were a noise, candy, kitchen utensil, food, cartoon character, animal, piece of furniture, texture, type of transportation, or other object. For each question, a member must think of an answer.

After asking the five questions, the guesser makes three guesses of who the mystery person is. Tell the guesser if he or she is right or wrong; give the answer if needed. Talk about the crazy questions and answers. Why did members answer the questions the way they did?

Long-term projects

You might spend time at one meeting brainstorming ideas. At the next meeting, divide the long-term project into smaller parts. Figure out what you will need to complete each part. Decide if everyone will work together on all of the parts, or if it would be better to work in small groups. If you want, you can make a schedule for your long-term project. But don't make this *too* rigid or formal, or it won't be fun anymore.

Make a mural

A mural is a long, continuous picture that is painted on a wall. To make a club mural you can work on at each meeting, find a long piece of paper. Mailing or poster paper on a roll works well. If you can't find any, tape pieces of typing or art paper together to make one long sheet.

Tack the mural paper on the wall and hand out markers, crayons, pens, and pencils. Ask members to draw pictures, doodle, or write thoughts on the mural at each meeting.

Members can add a drawing or note to the mural at each meeting until it's filled. At the end of the year, summer, or whenever you disband the club, divide the mural into sections and let each member keep a piece for a memento.

Prehistoric Painting

Murals are one of the oldest forms of art — they go back to the days when humans lived in caves and painted scenes on the walls. The earliest known murals are paintings of animals and were discovered in the caves of Spain and France. The ancient Egyptians also decorated the walls of tombs with scenes of wars, hunting trips, and ceremonies. *Mural* comes from the Latin word *murus,* which means *wall.*

Create a photo album

If a member has a camera, you can build a story about your club with photos. Ask someone who is not a member, or your sponsor, to take a group picture of all members at the first or second meeting. Take a few shots every time you meet or do activities outside of meeting time. Because you may not use up a roll of film quickly, record the picture number you took in the club notebook and make a note of what the picture was about. For example: "Picture 8 — January 7: Club built snowmen for fun. Had contest. Michelle won."

Once you develop your pictures, place them in order in a photo album (you can buy an inexpensive one at a discount store). Use your notes to label the photos in the album. If your club is ongoing from year to year — like a summer backyard club or a school club — creating a photo album is a great tool to get new members interested each year. Pass around the album at the first meeting. After seeing how much fun you've had in the past, new members will be eager to join.

Start a scrapbook

Just about anything can be placed in a club scrapbook. You can scribble notes, write poetry or stories, or trace your hands and sign them. You can tape or glue in your school pictures, things you collect together (such as leaves or movie ticket stubs), or articles and pictures from magazines and newspapers that interest you.

Although you can buy a scrapbook, it's just as easy to make one. Take an old three-ring binder, punch holes in some white or light-colored construction paper, and insert the paper into the binder. Decorate the cover with the club name or drawings.

Refreshments

It's fun to have something to eat and drink at your club meetings. You might decide to bring refreshments to every meeting or just serve them for special occasions. Either way, share the responsibility of providing refreshments and cleaning up.

How to decide who brings the goodies

Before you begin assigning treats, it's a good idea to record who will bring what and when. That way you'll be able to plan ahead, and you'll be less likely to forget. Use a calendar as a reminder or write down the information in your club notebook. Here are several ways to share the job of bringing refreshments.

Draw numbers

Write numbers on slips of paper, put them in a box or hat, and have everyone draw one. Make a list of the numbers and names in order. The first person on the list brings refreshments to the next meeting, the second person brings them to the meeting after that, and so on. Remind the members at each meeting whose turn is next.

Pair up

Share the work and expense by having one person bring drinks and another snacks. You can draw numbers and let the two people decide which duty they want.

Go potluck

One person volunteers to provide drinks, and everyone else brings anything they want to share with the group. Need some suggestions? You could bring a bag of cookies, crackers and cheese, a bag of popped popcorn, a jar of roasted peanuts, a box of fruit snacks, a bunch of bananas, a bag of bite-sized candies, a box of party mix, or small boxes of raisins.

"We have a summer club in our apartment complex that meets at the swimming pool. Usually my best friend and I bring the refreshments, and sometimes there are up to eighteen kids. My favorite things to bring are Popsicles, chips, Cheetos, and animal crackers." —Bryan

Recipes to try

You can find plenty of ready-made snacks in a grocery store or bakery, but sometimes it's more fun to make them from scratch.

This section includes many recipes to try. You can prepare them as club projects or by yourself to share with other members. Most aren't very complicated, don't require many utensils or dishes, and can be made ahead of time with little or no cooking. Some will have to be stored in a refrigerator or cooler. If you need to use a kitchen, get permission from a parent, sponsor, or other adult and don't be afraid to ask for help. If you have a home or backyard club, you'll have a kitchen nearby. Places of worship and community centers sometimes have kitchens you can use.

Personalized Pizzas

Nearly everyone likes pizza, and these small ones are very easy to make.

What you need

English muffins or plain bagels
margarine or butter
garlic powder
jar of pizza sauce
shredded cheddar cheese
grated parmesan cheese (optional)
oven mitts, plates, napkins

Optional Personalized Toppings:
cooked meats such as ham, pepperoni slices, or chicken
vegetables such as sliced mushrooms, sliced black olives, peppers, or tomatoes

What to do

Separate each muffin or bagel into two parts. Each side will be a little pizza crust. Lightly butter the slices and sprinkle them with garlic powder. Toast in a toaster oven on medium until light brown. If you don't have a toaster oven, toast the muffin or bagel in a toaster first, then spread the butter and sprinkle the garlic powder.

Spread a layer of sauce on each piece and top with cheese. If you want to add other toppings, put them on before the cheese. Broil in a toaster oven or regular oven. Watch them carefully. When the cheese melts, they're done. Sprinkle with grated parmesan cheese, if you want.

Club Subs

For a hearty club lunch, try this idea. You'll need to store any cheese, meat, and mayonnaise in a refrigerator or cooler.

What you need

sliced luncheon meat

fresh vegetables

sliced cheese

pickle slices

washed lettuce

mustard

mayonnaise

peanut butter

jelly or honey

sub or hoagie rolls

plates, napkins, utensils

small bowls (optional)

What to do

Place the ingredients on plates or in other serving dishes. If you wish, you can put the pickles, mayonnaise, mustard, and peanut butter and jelly in small bowls (or just open the jars and let people help themselves). Have everyone make their own subs.

Granola

Granola is a treat that energizes you. You can customize this recipe by adding other items you like. It's easy to mix together but takes 40 minutes to bake, so allow enough time. Because you'll need an oven to brown the granola, you might want to ask an adult to help.

What you need

4 cups oatmeal

1/2 cup flour

1/2 cup each of your choice:
  flaked coconut, sesame
  seeds, chopped nuts

1/2 cup vegetable oil

1/2 cup honey

1/2 cup raisins

1/2 cup dried fruit
  (such as pears, apples, or apricots)

1/2 cup chocolate chips
  or peanut butter chips

mixing bowls, large cookie sheet,
  oven mitts

spatula, large spoon

What to do

Place oatmeal and flour in a large mixing bowl. Stir to mix. Add 1/2 cup each of your choice of ingredients. In a small bowl, mix the oil and honey. Stir well for a minute or so. Pour the honey and oil mixture into the bowl containing the oatmeal and other ingredients. Stir until moist.

Spread the mixture on a large cookie sheet. Bake at 300° for 40 minutes. Every ten minutes, take out the sheet and use a spatula to carefully break up the mixture so it crumbles, browns, and gets crispy.

When it's done, remove from oven and add the raisins, dried fruit, and candy pieces. Let the granola cool, then place it in small baggies or one large plastic bag to share.

S'mores to Go

S'mores are fun to make around a campfire (make sure an adult is present if you have a campfire). If you can't have a fire, make these at home in a microwave oven and take them to your clubhouse.

What you need

one or two graham crackers per person

chocolate bars (one for every two people)

paper plates

marshmallow creme (comes in a jar and is located next to the marshmallows or in the baking aisle of a grocery store)

peanut butter (optional)

What to do

Carefully break the crackers in half and break up the chocolate bars. On each cracker half, place a few pieces of chocolate. Put the crackers and chocolate on a paper plate and microwave them on high for 1 1/2 to 2 minutes. Every oven is different, so check after 1 1/2 minutes. The chocolate should be slightly melted.

On the other cracker half, spread the marshmallow creme. Put this cracker on top of the chocolate one to make a s'more. Don't press down too hard, or you'll squeeze all the goodies out. Let cool.

For peanut butter s'mores, spread peanut butter instead of the marshmallow creme. For a triple sweet delight, spread more marshmallow creme and peanut butter on top of each s'more.

Place s'mores in a plastic sealed container or on a paper plate (cover well with plastic wrap or foil). The chocolate will harden when they cool, but the marshmallow creme and peanut butter will stay gooey.

Mix-and-Match Snack Attack

Many delicious dips and spreads don't need refrigeration until after they're opened. For this snack, either plan to finish all of the dips or bring a cooler for leftovers.

What you need

bag of tortilla chips or corn chips

bag of potato chips

bag of pretzels

carrot and celery sticks

beef sticks

can of bean dip

ranch dip

jar of picante dip or cheese spread

paper plates, plastic spoons

What to do

Pour the chips and pretzels onto paper plates. Place the carrot sticks, celery sticks, and beef sticks on another plate. Place the jars of dip within reach of everyone and put a spoon in each jar. Dig in!

Microwave Popcorn Balls

This is a snack you can make for your club ahead of time.

What you need

one bag of microwave popcorn
(plain or light butter)

1/4 cup (1/2 stick) butter or
margarine

3/4 cup sugar

1/4 cup water

1/4 cup light corn syrup

1/2 teaspoon salt

1/2 teaspoon vanilla

bowls, large spoon

plate or wax paper

What to do

Pop the popcorn in the microwave oven, according to the directions on the bag. Remove from the microwave; leave the bag closed and don't shake it (you want the unpopped kernels to stay at the bottom).

Place the butter or margarine in a small microwave-safe bowl and cook on high for 40 seconds or until melted. Mix all the ingredients except the popcorn in a medium-sized bowl and stir. Heat on high in the microwave for 3 to 5 minutes. Stop every minute and stir. The mixture will be ready when it has slightly thickened like syrup and has turned a light golden color. Carefully remove the mixture from the microwave oven. It'll be hot!

Open the popcorn and scoop it out into a large bowl. Remove any uncooked kernels. Pour the syrup over the popcorn. Stir with a large spoon to coat all pieces.

Butter your hands and form balls with the popcorn mixture. Press the pieces together to make them stick. Place the popcorn balls on a plate or wax paper. This recipe should make ten small or five large balls.

Peanut Butter Buffet

Peanut butter is a sticky but tasty treat. Have a peanut butter buffet at your next club meeting (but don't forget the napkins!).

What you need

jar of peanut butter

jar of jelly or jam

squeeze bottle of honey

bananas

apple slices

loaf of sliced bread

chocolate or vanilla cookies

plastic knives or spoons

lots of napkins

What to do

Open the jars and put a plastic knife or spoon in each. Peel and cut up several bananas. For fun, you might try cutting one in three chunks, splitting one lengthwise, and slicing a third into small pieces. Place the bananas on a paper plate with the apple slices. Place bread slices, cookies, and honey on the table near the other ingredients.

Now see how many combinations members can make. Here are some ideas: peanut butter and banana sandwich, apple slices with peanut butter spread, honey and peanut butter bread, fruit with honey topping, and cookies with peanut butter topping.

Raising Money for Your Club

Does your club want to buy T-shirts or hats? Do members want to attend a convention or fair? Do they want to help someone in need? Your club can successfully raise money for these and other reasons. All you need is a realistic project and a set of goals.

First, talk about why your club wants or needs the money. Set a club goal to earn a certain amount by a certain date. Then brainstorm ways to raise money. Do you want to ask people for donations or pledges, or do you want to raise money doing jobs, selling a product, or putting on a show?

For your fundraiser, consider forming committees. Committees are small teams of people (two or more) that plan a certain part of an activity. When you divide up a big job among committees, the work doesn't seem as hard. The committees meet and discuss their assignments, then report their ideas back to the club. Usually, committee members will also be the ones who do the work in their area.

The types of committees you'll need will depend on the way you choose to raise money. If you choose a bake sale fundraiser, for example, you'll need a baking committee to make the treats, an advertising committee to design posters and hand out flyers, and a sales committee to sell the food and collect the money.

Donation drives

If you're raising money for a good cause, you might be able to get the money by asking for donations (gifts of money).

But what's a good cause? A club skating party might sound like a wonderful cause to you, but you'll have a better chance of getting donations if you're raising money to help someone else. Cancer research or environmental action are examples of causes you could probably support with donations.

How to Start a Donation Drive

1. Learn about your cause and answer the following questions:
   - What is the problem?
   - Why do you need money?
   - Who will the money help?
   - How much time do you need to raise the money?
   - Where and when are you planning to use the money?

2. Form a committee to write a short speech about the cause, explaining the answers to the above questions. This is a speech members can use when they're asking for donations. If members practice the speech, they will sound and appear more confident.

3. Make collection containers for the money. You could use decorated coffee cans or shoe boxes.

4. Think about where you could go to ask people for donations. You could ask permission to set up a table in front of a grocery store or in the school halls. You could walk door-to-door in your neighborhood and ask for donations — if you do this, take a partner and have an adult walk with you. Be sure to thank those who donate.

Making a poster to track your progress

Record and watch your progress on a poster. Hang the poster in a public place. Seeing your goals and progress will encourage others to support your cause.

How to Make a Progress Poster

To make a poster, you'll need a large piece of white poster board and colored markers.

1. At the top of the poster, write a title and a short description of why you're raising money. Draw a rectangle below the description.

2. At the top of the rectangle, put your goal amount — the amount of money your club wants to raise. At the bottom, write $0.

3. Mark off small goals in between. For example, if your goal is to raise $100, mark the rectangle at $25, $50, and $75.

4. As you add money to the treasury, mark your progress in increments on the chart, making sure to record the date.

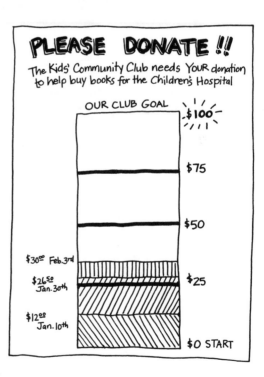

Pledges and "a-thons"

Clubs often use pledges, like donations, to make money to help others, but you can use pledges for other causes as well. When a person makes a pledge, he or she commits to pay a certain amount of money for each effort on your part. For example, Jump Rope for Heart is a popular pledge program in which people agree to pay a certain amount for every jump a participant makes.

Often pledge campaigns are called "a-thons" — such as marathons, walk-a-thons, read-a-thons, and swim-a-thons. You can invent an "a-thon" for almost any club, and it's better if the event is connected with the type of club you have. For example, an exercise club might have an aerobics-a-thon. As with collecting donations, talk about setting up committees to organize the parts of an "a-thon," including committees to organize participants and advertise the event.

Prepare what you'll say when you ask for pledges. Include some information about why you're raising money and how you'll use the money. Practice your pledge talk with other club members before you begin asking people to pledge. When you ask for a pledge, always include an option to simply donate money. Some people would rather give a known amount up front than wonder how much they'll have to pay later. Some people you talk to may not be interested in pledging. Don't feel bad if they say "no." Just try someone else.

After the event, contact the people who pledged money and collect the total due. You can show them your filled-out pledge sheet and tell them about the success of your event.

How to Make a Pledge Sheet

Before you ask for pledges, design a pledge sheet and make a copy for each member. You'll need a sheet of lined paper and a pen or pencil.

1. At the top of the paper, write the reason for the pledge.
2. Include a brief description of your pledge campaign.
3. Make columns for the pledgers' names, addresses, phone numbers, the amounts pledged per unit (such as miles walked), the total units you completed (such as total miles walked), and the total collected.

Save the Earth Walk-a-thon

The members of the Save the Earth Club will be holding a Walk-a-thon on Saturday, May 26, from 10:00 a.m. until 5:00 p.m. All proceeds will be donated to the Clean Up the Lakes Campaign in our city. Please help!

Pledge sheet

Name	Address	Phone	Amount Pledged Per Mile	Total Miles Walked	Total Collected

25 ways to raise money for your club

Service jobs

When you take out the trash or pull weeds in your yard, you're performing a service. Doing service jobs is a great way to raise money because people appreciate getting something in return for their contributions. Service jobs work especially well in home and backyard clubs or community center clubs. Following are some suggestions.

1. Clean and sweep out garages.
2. Baby-sit and pool the money.
3. Mow lawns and weed gardens.
4. House-sit while neighbors are away. Take in the mail, newspaper, and trash cans. Offer to water plants and feed pets.
5. Start a gift wrapping service for birthdays and holidays. Wrap an empty box as a sample. Charge a set price for small-, medium-, and large-sized presents. Have the customer supply the paper, bows, ribbon, and tape.

CLUB FLUB!

Your club was chosen to wrap 50 gifts for an end-of-the-year party at a retirement home. Unfortunately, you forgot to remove the price tags before wrapping the gifts!

When you're wrapping presents, remove the price tag on each gift first. Place the tags and any receipts you collect in an envelope. That way, you can return the receipt and price tag to the person who bought the present. To guarantee a happy customer, keep your work neat — and return any supplies you don't use.

6. Wash or walk the neighborhood dogs.

7. Gather together younger kids and teach them a skill, such as cheerleading, drawing, poetry, writing, or dance.

8. As a group, organize and run a neighbor's garage sale. Be prepared to clean items, price and label them, make sales, collect money, and carry items to customers' cars. For your payment, ask for a straight fee or a percentage of the profits.

9. Run a car wash. Car washes are a popular way to make money, so the competition might be strong. One way to get attention is by having a club member or two dress in an eye-catching way — clown suit, snorkel gear, formal wear, and so on. Another tactic is to offer extra services such as cleaning inside the car or including small baggies of potpourri to make the car smell good.

Sales

Many clubs at schools, places of worship, and community centers support their activities by selling items such as candy, holiday ornaments, gifts, and calendars. If you're interested, ask your sponsor to help you order the materials you'll need.

Making your own products to sell is a way to use your creativity. You might find your own unique product that fits your club perfectly.

"To make money in our club, we walked around the neighborhood and asked to paint people's faces. They were mostly friends or kids in the neighborhood. My mom is an artist, and she got us the paint. I have three brushes that are different sizes. The paintings were usually pictures of animals and hearts. We charged 25 cents for small paintings and 50 cents for large ones. One day we made two dollars, which we thought was pretty good." —Amy

10. For a craft club, sell the items you make.

11. Buy string and a variety of beads from a craft store and take orders for custom-made necklaces, bracelets, and anklets.

12. Tie-dye or hand paint new white T-shirts or caps and sell them.

13. Create hand-painted greeting cards for Hanukkah, Christmas, Kwanzaa, or any holiday.

14. Design book covers and paint or color them with markers.

15. Buy small plants and terra-cotta pots. Paint the pots in bright colors or use glitter paint. Add plants and sell to friends, neighbors, or teachers. Offer to customize the pots with the buyer's name.

16. Try a baked-goods stand stocked with homemade cookies or brownies.

17. Ask your parents and friends to donate old junk and hold a rummage sale.

18. Make gift wrap from sheets of brown or white mailing paper. Design with stencils, markers, rubber stamps, paints, or crayons to sell around the holidays.

19. Check into the recycling opportunities in your city. You may be able to sell donated aluminum cans or newspapers to a recycling center.

Performances

If your group likes performing, you can put on a show and raise funds. For any performance, you need to plan ahead. If you have a school, place of worship, or community center club, set a date and ask if you can use a stage, gym, or large room. If yours is a home or backyard club, stage your performance in a garage, backyard, or an open area of an apartment complex.

Brainstorm the things you'll need for your performance, such as props, costumes, and chairs for the audience. Form committees that can advertise, collect admission, and set up and remove chairs.

20. Put on a puppet show. Use a large cardboard box for a puppet theater. Cut a rectangular opening for the performance area. If you can't find one, turn a table on its side and hide behind it. The easiest puppets to make are ones from old socks. Add eyes and a mouth with markers, makeup, or buttons. Glue or staple fabric scraps, yarn, cotton, or tissues for the hair. Dress the puppets in doll clothes or drape fabric pieces around them and pin in place.

    You can find puppet scripts in books at the library, or follow a story from a book. Select one person to act as the narrator and read the story while the others read the speaking parts or dialogue.

21. Fashion shows can either be serious — such as ones showing off the new looks for the school year — or silly. Mix dancing with modeling or wear clothes or outfits that obviously don't match. Ask someone to be the emcee, or announcer, and describe the clothes. Play fun music in the background.

22. Create a clown act complete with funny clothes and makeup. Book performances at children's birthday parties.

23. If you have a sports club or if your members play sports, put on a sports exhibition. Members who skateboard, in-line skate, do gymnastics, jump rope, and ride bikes freestyle could show off their talents. Have members practice routines with music. Charge a small admission fee. You can make extra cash by selling cold drinks and popcorn.

24. Both actors and audiences enjoy a good melodrama. A melodrama is a simple play that includes a hero or heroine and a villain. In this type of play, the characters are exaggerated — the hero or heroine is very, very good and the villain is very, very bad. Find scripts for melodramas at your library or write your own. One characteristic of melodramas is that the audience cheers the hero or heroine and boos the villain. For extra fun, make bags of popcorn to sell to the audience.

25. Stage a variety show. Almost anything goes in this type of show: dancing, acting, juggling, performing magic tricks, singing, playing musical instruments, telling jokes, and performing pet tricks.

How to Stage a Variety Show

1. Write down the names of everyone who wants to participate.

2. Next to each name, write what type of act the member wants to perform. Try to get a variety of different acts. Members might even sign up for more than one. Schedule more acts than you think you need because some members might quit before the show goes on.

3. Count the number of acts you have. Each one will probably last two to three minutes, with one minute in between to change and announce the next performer. This means that fifteen acts will take about an hour to perform if everything goes smoothly.

4. Pick an emcee or announcer. This person won't perform in any of the acts but will have a list of the acts and the order in which they perform. Before each act comes on stage, the emcee announces the names of the performers. He or she also welcomes the audience at the beginning of the show and thanks them for coming at the end.

5. Performers can practice on their own at home, but your club should get all the acts together at least once before the show. At the final rehearsal, the emcee will run the show as if an audience is watching.

6. On the day of the show, have one or two people ready to set up chairs, the music, and the money box.

Advertising your product, service, or show

Once you've decided on a product to sell, a service to provide, or a show to put on, you'll need to let others know about it. Telling friends and neighbors about your event can be a successful way to advertise. If you're collecting donations or pledges, you can advertise your cause as you go door-to-door. There are other simple tools to advertise your club's fundraisers.

Flyers

Flyers can describe your club's project, product, or show. When you design a flyer, think about where you'll put the name of your club. Add information about the product or service you're offering, including why you're raising the money. If you're staging a performance, include the place, time, date, and admission charge. Hand-print your flyers or design them on a computer. Attract attention with brightly colored paper and drawings.

Ask permission to post your flyers on bulletin boards at your school, place of worship, or community center. If you hand them out door to door, use a rubber band to secure the flyers to the doorknobs.

RUMMAGE SALE!

Wilson School Science Club is having a sale to raise money for new computer software.

Please Come!

WHEN:
Saturday, October 25th
9:00 a.m.—4:00 p.m.

WHERE:
Wilson Intermediate
School Cafeteria

For More Information Call:
555-6970

Posters

Like flyers, posters are a great way to advertise. Decorate poster board with markers or poster paints. Use big letters and bold colors to attract attention. Include the same types of information recommended for the flyer.

You can hang posters on walls at your school, place of worship, or community center. (Get permission first.) Or, with a staple gun, attach your poster to a stake. (Have an adult help you with this.) Pick a popular spot and drive the sign into the ground.

Budgeting and managing your money

Let's say your Spanish club at school is planning a Mexican fiesta to raise money. Members suggest some exciting ideas: strolling mariachi musicians, a dinner with all the trimmings, even dancers with castanets. Word gets around school and everyone wants a ticket. But two weeks into working on the fiesta, your club realizes that the ticket sales won't be enough to fund all of your plans. You've managed to pay for the dancers, but there's not enough money left to buy the food — not even a burrito.

Whenever your club plans an event that costs money, you must make a budget in advance. A budget spells out exactly how you will use your money. It lists every item you want or need and how much it will cost. When you have a budget, you'll know what you can and can't afford, and you won't run out of money.

On the next page, you'll find a "Club Budget Chart" you can copy and use to organize your expenses for an upcoming event. You can budget as a group or in committees, or you may leave the responsibility to the treasurer. Here's how to fill in the chart:

1. At the top, write the event and the amount of money the club has available to spend. This amount may be all of the money in your treasury or just the portion you want to spend on the event.

2. In the first column, list all of the items you want to buy.

⭐ CLUB BUDGET CHART ⭐

Event: _____

_____

_____

_____

Amount of money available to spend: $_____*

Items Wanted	Cost of Items First try	Cost of Items Second try	Cost of Items Third try
1.	$	$	$
2.	$	$	$
3.	$	$	$
4.	$	$	$
5.	$	$	$
6.	$	$	$
7.	$	$	$
8.	$	$	$
Total Cost of Items	$	$	$

* **Note:** Don't forget to factor in sales tax for the items you plan to buy (ask your sponsor or another adult for help).

3. Find out how much each item will cost and write that amount in the second column. Check prices in catalogs or on store shelves, or ask your sponsor or another adult for help in checking prices. You may have to do some math at this point. If you're buying more than one of an item, you'll have to multiply the cost of the item by the number you want and then place the total in the second column. For example, if you want 24 miniature Mexican flags for your fiesta and they cost 20 cents apiece, you would multiply 24 flags x $0.20 to get $4.80 for that item.

4. Add up the costs in the second column and write the amount in the Total Cost of Items line. This is your first try. If the total is more than the amount of money you have to spend, you've gone over budget. Now the club will have to make decisions. You might decide to get rid of one item, buy less of an item, or shop for a better price.

5. Make your adjustments and try again in the third column. This is your second try. If you don't make your budget this time, keep adjusting until you do.

"During the summer, our club decided to sell lemonade and Kool-Aid to make money. I was in charge of buying the supplies – drink mix and paper cups. We had $19 in our treasury. My mom took me shopping, and we went to three different discount stores to get prices. I wrote down how much the items cost at all three stores, and then I bought the cheapest ones. I made sure that everything together cost less than $19.

"Managing money makes sense. It's using your brain. If your club doesn't manage the money you have, pretty soon you'll be broke." —Mark

10

Solving Club Problems

You've set up a club, voted on officers, and even had a first meeting — but now things aren't going so well.

Your club hasn't had any new members for a long time, and the regular members are getting bored.

You sense some problems forming in your club.

What can you do?

No matter how well you organize your club, you might still run into problems along the way. Some will be easy to solve, and others will be more difficult. When you realize that your club is heading for trouble, take time to confront the issue. Think about what you and the other members can do to solve the problem. Then take some time to learn from the situation — what can you do so this doesn't happen again? This chapter describes ten common problems other clubs have experienced and offers some solutions.

If you have tried everything and nothing seems to work, consider asking an adult for help. Your sponsor, youth leader, or a parent might see a solution you haven't yet thought of.

"How can we keep members interested in our club?"

One of the toughest problems in any type of club is keeping members coming back to the meetings. Often, joining is the exciting part, and after that members lose interest or become bored. So how do you overcome this problem? Use *incentives* — activities, games, rewards, and other things that draw members back to meetings.

Schools and businesses use rewards to encourage people to strive for goals. You might use club money to buy small items (such as colored pens, funny pins, stickers, or small pieces of candy) for members who attend every meeting the first month. Or use these rewards to recognize members who have worked especially hard for the club. You can also make your own rewards by cutting out medals or ribbons from construction paper and decorating them with glitter and your club emblem.

Be careful not to use rewards too often because they can seem like bribes. Members shouldn't be coming to meetings just to get rewards. Reread chapter 8 and use some of those ideas.

Another approach is to call or talk to the no-show members separately. Ask them what's bothering them about the club and what ideas they have to improve it. Invite them to present their ideas at the next meeting.

You might also want to make regular attendance one of your club laws, with a penalty for missing a meeting. You might state that if members miss a meeting, they must pay a small fine, such as five cents. You can make an exception for members who are sick, out of town, or who have another conflict. The money could go into the treasury or toward buying rewards for those who have perfect attendance at the end of the year or summer.

"Our members seem to be running out of energy, ideas, and enthusiasm. What can we do?"

Perhaps it's time to change the purpose of your club. If you feel that members no longer like your club's purpose, call for a club discussion and vote on a change of direction. Reread chapter 2 for ideas.

Depending on the type of club you have, you might be able to shift your purpose without changing your club completely. For example, let's say your after-school board game club has played every game the members own. It's nice outside and members want to play outdoor games and sports. Expand your club's purpose to playing all games, and play inside or out depending on the weather and the desire of the members.

"Some club members are starting to hang around together and ignore other members. What can we do?"

It's natural for a large group to divide into subgroups, but forming exclusive groups (called *cliques*) and excluding some members isn't good for the club. The whole idea of a club is to unite members for a common cause. If you see small groups forming, try the direct approach. Talk to each person in the group separately. Tell them you're worried about the club's unity. Ask them for ideas to help get the club spirit back and involve them in presenting their ideas to the club. Perhaps they feel that the other members aren't listening to their views or giving their ideas much credit.

If the direct approach doesn't work, try the indirect approach. Choose a project that requires a large effort from everyone — such as a fundraiser. Form committees by asking everyone to draw a number to decide which committee they'll serve on and state ahead of time that no one can trade numbers. The odds are that the members of the small group will each end up in different groups. This gives the people in the small group a chance to get to know and appreciate other club members.

What happens if neither approach works? Try organizing us-against-them competitions with other clubs. Play a weekly game of tug-of-war, basketball, or a board game. Give points to the club that wins and keep a running total. Encourage your club to unite and work as a team to win.

"Our leader isn't doing the job well at all. How can we fix this problem?"

If the club is running fine even with a weak leader, you might not need to take any action. Not everyone is a natural-born leader, but most people can sharpen their skills over time. If the other club officers or leaders are doing a good job, they might be able to set good examples. Members who haven't been elected to an office can help by suggesting ideas and volunteering for duties.

If a club leader is rude or bossy or never participates, talk to him or her about the problem. Ask your sponsor to come to the discussion to keep things calm and on track. Perhaps the leader doesn't realize how he or she is behaving.

If the leader doesn't want to change, you might have to ask for a recall vote. This is a vote to decide whether to remove the leader from office. To do this fairly, the majority (over half) of the members should sign a petition that states they want a recall vote. A person who is removed from office should still be allowed to stay in the club.

To avoid this problem in the future, write down a list of responsibilities for each leadership position, and have officials sign the list when they're elected. By signing the list, the leaders acknowledge that they understand their duties and agree to fulfill them. Use the list to point out any problems with your leader in the future. Also try setting up shorter terms of office and include an option to re-elect leaders.

"What can we do if some members of our club don't get along?"

When members don't get along, try to find out why. Once you know the problem, you can work toward a solution.

Communication is the key to solving problems. One way to get people talking is to use a talking stick. A talking stick can be a stick, ruler, broom handle, or any object set aside for this purpose. Whenever a member holds the talking stick, he or she can talk without interruptions. Have the quarreling members take turns holding the stick and explaining how they feel. As members talk, keep in mind that no one is either right or wrong. What's important is to find a way to get along.

"I've had to break up arguments in clubs a billion times. It works to say something nice to the person who is mad like, 'We think you're nice,' or 'We're all friends.' It makes them feel better and stops the fighting." —Michael

If the members need help talking to each other, or if they resort to name-calling or yelling, try peer mediation. This is the process of solving problems with rules and a third person. The mediator can be the same person every time or a different person. He or she should be able to listen without taking sides.

In order to make mediation work, everyone should agree to follow three rules:

1. No name-calling.
2. No physical contact.
3. No interrupting.

If a person breaks a rule, the mediator reminds him or her to follow the rule. Each person is allowed two reminders. If someone breaks a rule a third time, the mediator should stop and ask the person to leave the meeting, or get an adult to help.

Here are the steps to peer mediation:

1. The mediator states that he or she is going to mediate the disagreement.
2. The mediator chooses one member and asks, "What's wrong?"
3. The member describes the problem without interruption from other members. The mediator listens without saying anything.

4. Repeat steps 2 and 3 for all the members involved in the disagreement.

5. The mediator then asks each member, "What would you like to happen?"

6. The mediator repeats the answers.

7. The mediator then asks if members can agree to each other's requests. If they can, go to step 8. If they can't, repeat steps 5, 6, and 7 until a solution is found.

8. The mediator states the agreed-upon solution and everyone shakes hands.

Finding a solution may be more difficult than revealing the problem. When things get tough, look at the kind of problem the members have. Do they disagree about club matters? If so, the conflict isn't such a bad thing. It's good to have differing ideas in a club. Let the members express their view one at a time. Discuss the issue with all the members and take a vote on the ideas.

The problem may be a personal disagreement. Sometimes one member insults another without knowing it or meaning to. The insulted member might become angry and try to fight back. When the two members don't talk about the incident, the problem gets worse. In this case, mediate the problem quickly and ask the members to make up and shake hands.

Sometimes members simply dislike each other. In this case, pressing the two to talk about what's wrong might cause hurt feelings and make the problem worse. If mediation doesn't work, remind the fighting members that the strength of the club depends on everyone working together. Ask them to cooperate and to follow the club and meeting rules.

"Peer mediating can also work in a club. You can work out most problems without an adult. Have a club leader stop and ask the members what the problem is. Have the leader look them in the eye. It's important to make eye contact so you can hear and see what they are saying. Have the leader listen and then repeat what the members say, only make it shorter. Sometimes the members can't find a solution. In a club, other members could give ideas for a solution. If nothing works, you may have to get a grown-up to help." —Kerre

"One of our members disrupts the meetings on a regular basis. What can we do?"

If you're using parliamentary procedure, members know that they should raise their hand to be recognized. When the disruption occurs, the leader should call for order and remind the member of the rules. If you aren't using parliamentary procedure, reread chapter 7, "Running the Meetings," and consider following a certain order for each meeting.

If the member continues to disrupt, consider whether the member has had a chance to be heard. Are other members ignoring or snubbing him or her? The club leader should make sure the person has a say on an issue. If the leader learns that the member is being disruptive because of a conflict with another member, use mediation to work through the problem.

Some people disrupt a meeting to get attention or feel powerful. The club leader should try talking to the person in private and explaining how important he or she is to the club. The leader should say that members would like that person to stay in the club, but everyone must follow the rules. The leader might also assign the person a job or responsibility to make the member feel needed. Perhaps that member could be the sergeant-at-arms — the officer in charge of keeping order at the meetings. The disruptive member would have to learn the rules of order for a meeting and behave according to them.

Unfortunately, some people refuse to follow rules. If a member constantly disrupts others or becomes violent, the leader might have to ask him or her to leave the meeting and even to leave the club.

"How can we keep in contact with members who move away?"

It's tough on everyone when a club member moves away. To keep in contact, you might create a monthly letter about the club's activities to send to the person who has moved away. Have all of the other members sign the letter. Some members might offer to be pen pals with the person and keep him or her up-to-date on club events. If the person returns for a visit, invite him or her to a special meeting.

Your club could also grant the person a charter to start a similar club in his or her new community. The new club can share the same goals and even the same name. Make copies of your filled-in "Club Plans," "Club Charter," and "Club Goals" and give them to the member who is leaving at a special going-away meeting. Include copies of the blank forms (see pages 7, 13, and 42) so the members of the new club can fill them out. To make things official, you can write this sentence at the top of the blank "Club Charter" form:

The members of the _____
(CLUB NAME)

club in _____ *grant our member* _____
(YOUR CITY OR TOWN)   (LEAVING MEMBER)

this charter to start a branch club in _____.
(NEW CITY OR TOWN)

Once the person has formed the new club, members of both clubs can communicate by writing letters and sharing news and photos.

"Our fundraiser was a flop. Now what can we do?"

First, don't panic. Almost everyone fails in one way or another before they succeed. But don't just dismiss the failure either. Talk about it with the other members. Don't blame anyone; learn from the failure. Use it to decide what *not* to do next time.

For example, instead of saying, "It was Kelly's idea. It was her fault we lost money on the project," say, "Kelly's idea was good, but it was more than we could do in such a short period of time. Next time, let's choose something simpler."

If club members are very sad or upset, don't try the same project again right away. To regain club spirit, brainstorm another idea and start planning. Make the new fundraiser or project small and simple — something you feel the club can tackle easily. Once you've succeeded with the small and simple project, members will feel confident again. They'll be ready to retackle the first project or try another larger or more complex one.

"Help! We're running out of money. What can we do?"

If the total in your club treasury is shrinking, stop spending money immediately. Look at what's left and brainstorm how you can use it to make more. Perhaps you could use the money that's left to create flyers to attract new members to your club (this works when members pay dues). If your club has never collected dues, now might be a good time to start. See page 43 for ideas.

To get members interested in raising money, set a goal. On a piece of poster board, write the amount you want to earn, along with a picture or description of what you plan to buy with the money. Hang it where everyone can see it. Reread chapter 9 for suggestions on ways to reach your goal.

"Our club is running out of steam. How can we get it going again?"

First, decide why your club is slowing down. If members aren't showing up for meetings, reread chapters 8 and 10 for ideas on making meetings more fun for everyone. If your club needs a new purpose, reread chapter 2 for suggestions on finding a focus.

Perhaps members are just bored — in that case, try shaking things up. Have a different member bring an activity idea or game to each meeting. Change the meeting location or make something fun to decorate the meeting room or give to members. Set new goals and challenge members with an exciting project. Invite new members to join — they can bring fresh ideas and renewed energy to the club.

If none of these ideas work, it might be time for the club to end. Don't get discouraged, however. Think about the good things that happened in your club. Reread chapter 1 and form a new club. Find friends who share your dream and start over.

Index

About the Author

Melissa Maupin is a graduate of Texas A&M University Corpus Christi with a B.A. in Communications and teacher certification in drama, dance, and physical education. Over the last nine years, she has taught and directed children of all ages in public school, day camps, and fine arts programs.

Melissa worked as a staff reporter for a regional newspaper and since that time has written dozens of articles for regional and national publications. She specializes in educational, ecological, and nature writing.

As a child, Melissa started and joined numerous clubs in her neighborhood and school and now helps her two sons and their friends with their clubs. She also teaches children as a volunteer for the fine arts programs at her son John Michael's elementary school. Melissa lives with her husband and children in Corpus Christi.

MORE BOOKS FROM FREE SPIRIT

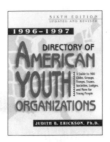

1996–1997 DIRECTORY OF AMERICAN YOUTH ORGANIZATIONS
A Guide to 500 Clubs, Groups, Troops, Teams, Societies, Lodges, and More for Young People

by Judith B. Erickson, Ph.D.

The most comprehensive guide available to adult-sponsored, nonprofit youth organizations in the United States, the *Directory* points young people toward hundreds of possibilities for fun, friendship, social action, and self-esteem. Ages 6–18.
$21.95; 200 pp.; softcover; 7 1/4" x 9 1/4"; ISBN 1-57542-001-5

THE KID'S GUIDE TO SOCIAL ACTION
How to Solve the Social Problems You Choose — and Turn Creative Thinking Into Positive Action

by Barbara A. Lewis

Everything kids need to make a difference in the world: step-by-step directions, forms, addresses and phone numbers, and inspiring true stories about real kids. Ages 10 and up.
$14.95; 208 pp.; softcover; B&W photos and illus.; 8 1/2" by 11"; ISBN 0-915793-29-6

THE KID'S GUIDE TO SERVICE PROJECTS
Over 500 Service Ideas for Young People Who Want to Make a Difference

by Barbara A. Lewis

Hundreds of ideas for all kinds of service projects, from simple ones anyone can do to large-scale commitments that involve whole communities. Ages 10 and up.
$10.95; 184 pp.; softcover; 6" x 9"; ISBN 0-915793-82-2

THE BEST FRIENDS BOOK
True Stories about Real Best Friends, Fun Things to Do with Your Best Friend, Solving Best Friends Problems, Long-Distance Best Friends, Finding New Friends, and More!

by Arlene Erlbach

Delightful stories, photographs, and activities celebrate friendship. Ages 9–13.
$10.95; 96 pp.; softcover; B&W photos and illus.; 6" x 9", ISBN 0-915793-77-6

To place an order, or to request a free catalog of SELF-HELP FOR KIDS® materials, write or call:

Free Spirit Publishing Inc.
400 First Avenue North, Suite 616
Minneapolis, MN 55401-1730
toll-free **(800)** 735-7323, local **(612)** 338-2068
help4kids@freespirit.com